" UNDERSTANDING TRADE UNIONS
Yesterday and Today "

Gerry McNamara, Kevin Williams, Des West
ICTU

Cartoons by

Martyn Turner

O'BRIEN EDUCATIONAL
DUBLIN

First published 1988 by O'Brien Educational Ltd.,
20 Victoria Road, Dublin 6, Ireland
in association with the Irish Congress of Trade Unions.
Copyright © Irish Congress of Trade Unions

Photo credits: Lensmen pp4, 110 (t&b), 112, cover; Wexford Engineering Company
ltd., 13 (t); TUC Library 13 (b), 18, 24 (t&b); National Library 19 (t), 52 (b);
ITGWU 19 (b); The Royal Society of Antiquaries of Ireland 22; G.A. Duncan 27, 38,
47, 52 (t); RTE Library 30, 115; National Museum 33 (t); Daily Mirror 33 (b);
Rex Roberts Studios ltd 54; Beryl Stone 61 (t&m), 96, 104 (b), 123; Eamonn
O'Dwyer (report) 61 (b), 142, cover; Tony Parkes 65 (t), 70 (t), 104 (t);
FWUI 70 (b); Derek Speirs (report) 65 (b), 83 (b); The Irish Times 83 (t);
Brian Farrell 84, cover; IDA 105 (t), cover; FAS 105 (b); Frank Fennell 121;
The Evening Herald 135 (t); Irish Wheelchair Assoc. 135 (b).
(t=top, m=middle, b=bottom of page.)

Typesetting: Phototype-Set Ltd., Dublin
Printing: Irish Elsevier Ltd., Shannon

BEV

5.13

Contents

Foreword

Hardly a day passes without the ICTU Information Office getting several queries from young people. Most of the questions are very simple. How can I join a union? Can I be sacked for joining? Should I be paid extra for working on bank holidays? Do I have to use a broken ladder? What is the rate of pay for hairdressers? Should I get a pay slip with my wages? What is a closed shop?

Any sixteen-year-old could tell you all about the Statutes of Kilkenny but nothing about the statutory minimum wage. School leavers know more about the courts of Henry VIII than they do about the Labour Court. They are often more familiar with the historic affairs of kings and princes than the heroic struggles of Larkin and Connolly. An historical perspective from the point of view of ordinary working people should help to put the record straight.

Ignorance of the world of work leaves young people vulnerable in the workplace. Unawareness of trade unionism deprives them of the support available to help them to help themselves. Teachers are not to blame. The educational system, the school curricula and the study materials available do not equip school leavers for life in the workplace.

School leavers know how to do well at interviews, but when they do get the job it is often a case of learning the hard way. Successful efforts are now being made to prepare our young people for handling human relations. Industrial relations remains a question of trial and error, mostly error.

The Irish Congress of Trade Unions hopes that *Understanding Trade Unions* will help to fill a conspicuous gap in our educational system. We are confident that this book will be of assistance to pupils, teachers, parents and young people already at work or about to start work.

Congress presented Gerry McNamara, Kevin Williams and Des West with a hefty tome of weighty material, full of industrial relations procedures, organisational structures and a fair amount of trade union jargon. They are practising teachers and experienced writers of educational materials. We are grateful for their hard work which has resulted in a book that is easily read and understood. Martyn Turner's cartoons, as always, spare no one's sensitivities in getting to the heart of the matter. I must point out that the characters he depicts are genuinely fictitious, despite their close resemblance to some of my

friends. Oliver Donohoe, our Research and Information Officer, coordinated the entire project, seeking out material and illustrations from an immense variety of sources, all of whose cooperation we deeply appreciate.

Without the customary high standards of professionalism and considerable patience of O'Brien Educational, we wouldn't have a book of which all concerned can be justifiably proud.

Peter Cassells
February 1988

Introduction

For years many teachers have felt that their pupils should be taught something about trade unionism and industrial relations. The lack of suitable material on the subject has often discouraged teachers from addressing these areas in class. It is precisely in response to the demand for such material that the Irish Congress of Trade Unions is publishing *Understanding Trade Unions*. This book is designed specifically to meet the demands of teachers for a suitable text on the subject. This initiative by ICTU is all the more timely in view of the inclusion of units on trade unionism and on industrial relations in the Transition Year Option and in the Vocational Preparation and Training Programme. This book also provides suitable material for the course in Social and Political Studies as recommended by the Curriculum and Examination Board.

Format of the Text

The book itself is written in the form of short chapters, each followed by a comprehensive and detailed series of questions, most of which are based on the preceding text. The questions are graded in terms of relative difficulty, and include multiple choice and true/false questions. Some require short factual answers, while others encourage a discursive approach. It is hoped that, in this format, the text can be used with classes of different ages and abilities. Each chapter can be covered in a forty-minute lesson period but can also be exploited in a further lesson or lessons. As the chapters constitute independent units, teachers need cover only the chapters of their choice.

Specialised terms are explained both in the body of the text and in an alphabetical glossary. This means that where the meaning of a term is forgotten, students do not have to search back through previous chapters but can refer directly to the glossary. The text can be used by any teacher, whether or not s/he has any prior knowledge of the subject matter. All that is required is that s/he read each chapter, and in particular the questions on it, before presenting it to a class.

Target Groups

The text is designed to accommodate students at both junior and senior cycles — and indeed may also be used in Adult Education courses and in courses for trade union members. Here we would emphasise the importance

Congress attaches to providing some background in trade unionism to early school leavers. Study of the key chapters, especially 'Joining Up' and 'Taking Part', should be an essential part of the education of this constituency of the educationally (and usually socially) deprived. More generally, it is worth pointing out that the text contains a considerable section on the history of the trade union movement, and so should also prove useful to teachers of history. It will, ICTU hopes, prove enlightening to students to be presented with a perspective on historical events from the point of view of ordinary working people, rather than that of influential and powerful classes and individuals. More specifically, and on an even more practical note, it is hoped that the history section will provide material for a Special Topic question in Leaving Certificate Honours history. Similarly, it is hoped that several of the chapters on the organisation and function of trade unions and on labour law can be used by teachers of Business subjects. *Understanding Trade Unions* will, however, no doubt be of most value to teachers of Social Education programmes, of the Transition Year Option and of the Vocational Preparation and Training Programme, and to school Guidance Counsellors. It should also provide appropriate resource material for the Industrial Relations topic in the creative alternative Leaving Certificate being developed by the Shannon Curriculum Development Unit.

EDUCATION IN TRADE UNIONISM — A CONCEPTUAL FRAMEWORK

As authors, we were at all times conscious that education in trade unionism has an essential place in any programme of social education which aims to prepare young people for working life.[1] We would argue that education in trade unionism is part of education in community responsibility, it is part of civic or political education in the broad sense. Through such education young people should become aware of the capacity they have to control their own lives and to influence the way their society is organised. After all, the arrangements which provide for the exercise of power in society do not derive from the dictates of immutable natural law, but are prescribed by laws made by people. One of the ways people can influence the nature of these laws and thereby assume a voice in the ordering of social life is through active participation in their trade union. This involvement is also a form of social education in that it can help to make people aware of the necessity to attend to the welfare of the less fortunate, both in Ireland and abroad.

Trade Unionism and Industrial Relations

It is also important to appreciate that the study of trade unionism will help young people to come to a better understanding of the whole area of industrial relations. For this reason the questions at the end of most chapters include fictional case studies suitable for role-play/dramatisation, and several separate longer case studies are also provided. These enable students to realise the importance of good human relations in the workplace. By means of such role-play students can explore the implications and consequences of different possible strategies in response to the problems set in the case studies. In this manner we would hope that they would come to see that, at least in some circumstances, sensitive and enlightened attitudes can prevent disputes arising.

The Case Study Method

On a methodological note we should point out that making use of case studies does not necessarily involve role-play. For example, students can be divided into small discussion groups with rapporteurs from each group presenting short reports to the full class group. These reports provide a summary of the conclusions or disagreements of each group. This can be followed by a general discussion in which the teacher tries to make an overall appraisal of different approaches to the incident.

Teachers should not, however, be at all apprehensive about using role-play in the classroom, or at the prospect of making short audio or video playlets.[2] Where space permits, the ideal is to divide a class into small groups with each preparing its own version of the incident which it then presents to the rest of the class. Students and teachers will be amazed at how different groups understand and dramatise the same situation. Alternatively, the teacher can choose a different group each week to prepare a particular sketch and, if possible, allow the students a few minutes on their own to prepare a version of the incident. While the group is preparing its sketch the teacher continues a general discussion with the rest of the class. Teachers will find that pupils greatly enjoy and profit from such activity.

Other Educational Resources

Finally, we would point out that *Understanding Trade Unions* is only one instrument which can be used in teaching about trade unionism. Teachers can also invite speakers from Congress and thereby give their students an opportunity to listen to and discuss matters with those directly involved. Use could also be made of such films as *F.I.S.T.*, *Blue Collar*, *Rosie the Riveter*, *Union Maids*, or *The Molly Maguires*. Shorter films such as *The Trouble with Archie*, *Ursula Joins the Union* (available from Local Government and Public Services Union) or *Where's the Satisfaction?* are particularly appropriate in teaching about industrial relations.[3] In teaching about the trade union movement a teacher with an interest in folk or contemporary music could make use of recordings on the subject by various artistes. Education in trade unionism and industrial relations can, therefore, be a fascinating and enriching exploration of human affairs.

Notes

(1)   For further information on the theme of preparation for working life, readers should see Kevin Williams and Gerry McNamara, *The Vocational Preparation Course: An Educational Appraisal and Practical Guide*, Dublin: Association of Secondary Teachers, Ireland, 1985, Chapter VI.

(2)   For advice on such work see *ibid*, Chapter V, part 2.

(3)   Teachers who require information regarding suitable films/videos should contact the Film Education Officer, Irish Film Institute, Harcourt Street, Dublin 2 or the Information Officer, ICTU, 19 Raglan Rd., Dublin 4.

1 · Early days of the Labour Movement

TRADE UNIONS FOR THE UNSKILLED

The year 1889 is an important year in the history of the trade union movement. In that year, the first effort to organise unskilled workers into unions began. Craft unions had been active in Ireland for at least one hundred and fifty years before that but these had been largely for skilled craftsmen such as carpenters, tailors and so on. By 1890 only about 17,500 workers were members of a union. This was only a small part of the workforce and was made up mostly of skilled men. Unskilled workers were unorganised and had no one to speak for them.

The slow growth of Irish trade unionism before 1890 can be explained in a number of ways:

- There were few factories in Ireland, except in Ulster, and the number of unskilled workers was fairly small.

- In the last century politics in Ireland were very much taken up with the land question because the great majority of Irish people lived on the land. As a result the terrible conditions of working-class people in the towns and cities were ignored.

- The most important reason why trade unionism was slow to get going was the opposition of employers. Most employers were completely against trade unions because they saw them as interference with their right to run their companies and were afraid that they would have to pay more to their workers and give more time off, pensions etc. They were quick to sack anyone who joined a union and with so many unemployed it was easy to get new workers.

Not surprisingly workers were slow to join.

Organising a trade union was also a dangerous activity. Union organisers could easily be sacked and in Ireland, one hundred years ago, with no dole or social welfare to fall back on, the loss of a job meant even worse poverty for a family than that in which they already lived. The serving of strike notice by a union was often followed by the employers' sacking all the workers and hiring replacements from the huge numbers of unemployed desperate for a job. A lost strike could mean all the workers being sacked, or at best having to come back on the employer's terms. Among the unskilled, with masses of unemployed waiting to take the jobs of strikers or sacked workers, joining a trade union took courage.

EMPLOYERS v. UNIONS: THE STRUGGLE BEGINS

By 1900 the organisation of unskilled workers was increasing steadily and a number of big and successful strikes in England — the London dockworkers' strike, the strike of the women workers in the match factories — proved to unskilled workers in Ireland that strike action and support between unions could bring big improvements in their working and living conditions. Unions representing general labourers, such as the National Union of Dockworkers, grew fast and by 1900 unions which were members of the Irish Trade Union Congress had more than 60,000 members.

The unions were getting strong enough to take on the employers to get better wages and conditions for their members, but the employers were not going to give in without a fight. In many cases the employers, often supported by the police and the army, attacked striking workers and broke up pickets. To end disputes they also used strike-breakers, who were sometimes brought in from other parts of the country. These tactics caused some terrible clashes; the right of the workers to join a union if they wished had to be fought for town by town — Belfast 1907, Dublin 1908, Cork 1909, Wexford 1911. The Wexford dispute was typical of many others.

The Wexford Lock-out

In 1911 two factory owners in Wexford decided to close down their companies, locking out 550 workers, because they joined the Irish Transport and General Workers' Union. They had made no demands on the employers or created any trouble. The local organiser of the union, P. T. Daly, said that the union would agree to the men joining another union if that was what the men and the employers wanted. The employers refused to discuss the matter and would not agree to accept the right of the workers to be in any union. Two hundred and fifty extra policemen were sent to the town and Daly was beaten unconscious with clubs by a local factory owner and a local newspaper editor. Other employers in the area joined with those who had locked-out their workers and closed down their factories, where the workers were members of the ITGWU. It was an all-out effort to smash the union in Wexford town. There were clashes between the police and the workers and the police used their batons without mercy. One worker was killed during a police baton charge and many others were injured. The union leader, Daly, was arrested

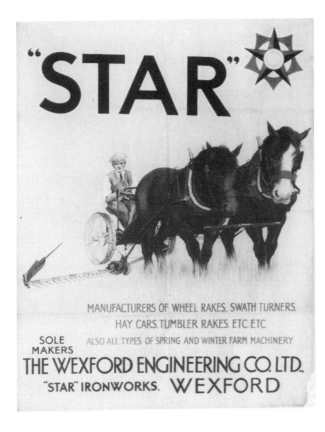

"STAR"

MANUFACTURERS OF WHEEL RAKES, SWATH TURNERS,
HAY CARS, TUMBLER RAKES. ETC. ETC.

SOLE MAKERS   ALSO ALL TYPES OF SPRING AND WINTER FARM MACHINERY.

THE WEXFORD ENGINEERING CO. LTD.

"STAR" IRONWORKS. WEXFORD

left: An advertisement from the Wexford company involved in the lock-out.

below: In the nineteenth century employers opposed the introduction of laws that would prevent them employing children. Conditions for children were very harsh — they often worked over fifty hours a week in tough and unhealthy situations.

and sent to prison but James Connolly was sent to take over the leadership and the workers stood firm. The employers were losing money and were now more willing to listen to the men. Connolly suggested that the workers should set up a new union, called the Irish Foundry Workers' Union, which would be related to the ITGWU. The employers accepted this deal, although everyone knew that the 'new union' would be a branch of the ITGWU. Shortly after, it became officially part of the Transport Union. The outcome of the Wexford lock-out was a great victory for the trade union movement. The union had survived an attempt to wreck it, and the workers had forced the employers to accept the right of workers to be members of any union they wanted.

The Taff-Vale Case

Although the trade union movement won a series of disputes similar to the Wexford one, the employers still resisted the spread of trade unionism among their workers. They turned to the law, and began to take the unions to court. The courts were sympathetic to the employers and many decisions were given against the trade unions. The worst of these judgements from the union viewpoint came in 1900 when the Railwaymen's Union in England refused to carry blackleg labour on its way to break a strike at the Taff Vale Railway Company. After the strike the company took the Railway Union to court, seeking compensation for the money lost during the dispute. The court ordered the union to pay the company £30,000. This was a disaster for the labour movement: it meant that any union that went on strike, even if it won, could be ruined by having to pay compensation for money lost during the strike. It also meant that a union could be made to pay for anything an official or even an ordinary member did. No union could afford to strike under these circumstances.

The unions at once began to campaign to have the law changed, and after a long struggle the government was forced to bring in the Trade Disputes Act in 1906. This Act, which is still law in Ireland, protected unions' money from legal action, defined what a trade dispute means and allowed workers to picket peacefully. This meant that the unions were once again free to take industrial action without the risk of being taken to court, and a new wave of confidence spread through the movement. However the struggle to force the employers to accept the right of workers to be in a union was really only starting, and over the next few years it was to be war to the death, particularly in Dublin.

14

Questions

1. Finish the sentences:
   (a) Craft unions represented skilled workers such as . . . . .
   (b) There were few industries in Ireland, apart from . . . . .
   (c) By 1890 only 17,500 workers were . . . . .

2. (a) Why is 1889 an important year in trade union history?
   (b) Why were employers against the spread of trade unions?
   (c) What did the employers do to try to stop workers joining a union?
   (d) Why was the Wexford lock-out important to the ITGWU?
   (e) What was the importance of the Taff Vale Case?
   (f) What rights were given to trade unions under the Trade Disputes Act of 1906?

3. Why did it take courage for unskilled workers to join a union?

4. The Trade Disputes Act of 1906 gives legal protection to trade unions. Why could the trade unions not take strike action without this Act?

Discussion

Should trade unions have to pay for the losses of a company where strike action has been taken? List the arguments: (1) an employer, (2) a trade union official, might make about this matter.

2 · The Turn of the Century

IRISH TOWNS AFTER THE FAMINE

There was little industry in Ireland, other than in Ulster, and most Irish towns and cities were centres of trade and public administration. In the years after the famine the towns grew very slowly; for example, the population of Dublin rose from 317,000 in 1851 to only 404,000 in 1911. The only Irish city to show rapid growth was Belfast, which grew from 75,000 in 1841 to 400,000 by 1900. This growth was caused by the arrival of thousands of people from the countryside, looking for employment in the fast-growing shipbuilding and linen industries.

Outside Belfast and Derry there were few jobs to attract people to the cities and towns and the sons and daughters of farmers, for whom there was no land available, had to go to America or to the cities of England to earn a living. The numbers who had to emigrate from Ireland were huge — it was like an open wound draining away the young blood of the country.

Types of Employment Available

For those that stayed there was very little steady employment and wages were low. The coming of the railways brought quick growth in the numbers working in transport. Men worked not only in the railways but as carters and labourers hauling goods in horse carts from the railway stations to nearby villages. Other important sources of jobs were as domestic service and farm labouring. In 1891 there were 250,000 girls working as maids, cleaners, and cooks; domestic service was the only job for a young country girl who had to leave home and look for work in a town. These servants were the most badly paid group of workers. In 1879 the average maid was paid about £10 a year, about 4 shillings (20p) a week. (An industrial worker earned about 90p a week.) For this she worked long hours (6.30 in the morning to 10.30 at night was not unusual) and time off was hardly known at all.

Farm labourers were the largest group of male workers. By 1900 they were paid about 10 shillings (50p) a week. This type of work was very uncertain, depending on weather and time of year, and there could be long periods of unemployment. Many farm labourers had to go to England and Scotland for part of the year to find work.

SKILLED AND UNSKILLED WORKERS

The living standards of industrial workers depended on whether they were skilled or unskilled. The skilled man, like a cooper (barrel-maker) or a carpenter, was usually a member of a craft union, which kept down the numbers coming into the trade and so protected employment and kept wages up. Unskilled workers were not organised into unions until the end of the century and even then the large number of unemployed labourers kept wages very low.

In general about one worker in five was skilled and the difference between the wages for skilled and unskilled people was large. For example, in 1914 a skilled worker such as a carpenter earned about 37s. 6d (£1.85) per week compared with about £1 per week for an unskilled carter or docker. For general labourers short-time working and regular periods of unemployment were usual. Whatever work there was for general unskilled labourers was usually 'casual' — that is, men were hired for one day or one week at a time. An example of this 'casual' work was that of the Dublin dock labourers, who had to queue every morning outside the dock gates while the employers picked whatever men they wanted. This meant that a worker did not know if he would have a job next week, or even next day. There were always too many general labourers looking for too little work, and anyone who gave trouble to an employer, by joining a union for example, could be easily sacked.

WORK FOR WOMEN AND CHILDREN

Jobs for women and children were almost impossible to find except in Ulster, where many of both were employed in the linen industry. This was poorly paid and unhealthy work; the pay for a woman was about 12 shillings (60p) a week in 1906, and the warm damp conditions in the factories caused the spread of diseases like tuberculosis. Workers were often made to pay fines for being late or for singing at work. Outside Ulster there was little work; women sometimes worked as cleaners or took in washing, while children were employed as messengers or assistants to tradesmen but were let go as soon as they were old enough to be paid full wages. For boys the usual option at this stage was to join the British Army.

HOUSING CONDITIONS

The typical working-class family in an Irish large town lived in a tenement, one or more rooms in a large old house which was shared with many other families. Most families had to live in the centre of the town to be close to places of work such as the docks, because regular trips by train or tram were

Some of the few hundred match workers at Bryant and Mays' who struck, won their case and organised their own union in 1888. That same year a Miss Black suggested to the Trade Union Congress 'that in trades where women do the same work as men, they shall receive equal payment.'

top: The Irish Women Workers' Union.
below: The Irish Citizen Army in training, 1915.

too expensive. Largely because of shortage of money, corporations and town councils made little effort to improve housing conditions. The very small rents which most families could afford discouraged landlords from spending any money on improving the houses. In most cases many families would share one toilet and one tap, often situated in the back yard.

In smaller towns the typical working family lived not in a tenement but in a small three-roomed cottage, but living conditions were much the same. Only in Belfast and Derry did the urban workers have decent housing; rows and rows of two-bedroomed houses with parlour, kitchen scullery and a tiny back yard with a toilet were available at half the rent of a similar house in Dublin. This was because the shipyard and linen industries provided secure employment and many families had two incomes, with both spouses working.

Questions

1. Finish the sentences:
    (a) The average wage for a skilled worker in 1914 was . . . . .
    (b) Tuberculosis spread in the linen factories because . . . . .
    (c) The work of a carter was . . . . .
    (d) The life of a maidservant was hard because . . . . .

2. (a) Why did so many people emigrate from Ireland after the famine?
    (b) Why did Belfast grow faster than other Irish cities?
    (c) What were the main types of employment available for unskilled workers?
    (d) What was the difference between skilled and unskilled workers?
    (e) Why was it so difficult to organise unskilled workers into unions?
    (f) What was 'casual' labour?
    (g) What were the main types of work available for women and children?
    (h) In what sort of house did the typical working-class family live?

3. (a) Is there a wider choice of jobs for: (a) skilled, (b) unskilled workers today?
    (b) List jobs that are: (a) skilled, (b) unskilled.
    (c) Find out where and for how long a person has to train for each job on your list of skilled jobs.
    (d) Is there a difference in pay between skilled and unskilled workers?

4. Compare housing conditions today with those of one hundred years ago. List the things that have changed.

Discussion

Would you rather have lived in an Irish town in 1900 than in one today? What things have changed?
Are there any ways in which life was better in 1900?

3 · *Dublin City*

SLUM TENANTS

The living conditions of Dublin's working-class in the early years of the twentieth century were more like those of a city in India than any other large North European town. According to the census of 1901 the population was just over 400,000; of these nearly one quarter lived in the city centre tenements. These tenements had been built around 1750-1780 as houses for wealthy families, but as the wealthy left the city to live in suburbs, they were gradually let out to poorer people with up to ten families occupying each house.

About 80 per cent of the families in the city, more than 20,000, lived in only one room, while another 5,000 had only two rooms. An inquiry into housing conditions in Dublin in 1914 reported that 37,500 people lived in houses which were unfit for human habitation, and a further 23,000 people lived in houses which were not only unfit for human habitation but 'incapable of being rendered fit'. Often, as many as ninety people had to use one tap in an outside yard and it was common to find only one toilet, which was also used by people passing by on the street. Of the 5,000 tenement houses, more than 1,500 were condemned buildings, needing demolition. Indeed, in September 1913, two four-storey tenements collapsed killing seven people and injuring dozens.

Death and Disease

These housing conditions produced an appalling state of public health. Out of every 1,000 babies born each year in Dublin, 152 died before they were a year old, compared with ninety-five per thousand in the rest of Ireland. About 201 of the 9,000 deaths registered in Dublin in 1911 were of babies under one year of age.

In 1911 the death rate in Dublin was 27.61 per cent per thousand people per annum, compared with a figure of less than 27 per cent for Calcutta, a city notorious for being infested with diseases such as cholera. The great killer disease was tuberculosis or consumption, for which no cure existed, and which killed 1,414 people in 1913 alone. TB was particularly tragic because it mainly took the lives of young people and it was directly related to overcrowded living conditions. The poor sanitation and toilets in the

above: At Summerhill, near Gardiner Street, a group of mostly barefoot children stands with a woman. Deaths of children under the age of one year accounted for 20 per cent of deaths in the city. In 1913, they accounted for more than 25 per cent due to lack of food and heat because of the lock-out.

below: The bare floorboards and scant furniture of this room on Newmarket Street were typical of Dublin tenements. A half-eaten loaf of bread lies on the table while cooking utensils are strewn across the floor. Clothes hang to dry near the fireplace, the family's only source of heat.

tenements gave rise to other diseases and it is not surprising that the dreadful living conditions were seen as being directly responsible for more than one-third of all deaths in Dublin city.

In these conditions drunkenness and prostitution flourished as people tried to forget their misery and improve their incomes. O'Connell Street and Grafton Street were crowded with unfortunate girls from the slum districts. Soon after he came to Dublin, Jim Larkin asked, 'If Dublinmen are so proud of the city, why did they not look after the little children who were running about their streets, hungry and dirty and badly clothed?'

Low Wages

And what of wages? The average wage for a tenement dweller was about 90p per week. On average this would have been spent as follows: rent 12½p; fuel and light 10p; food 52½p; thus leaving 15p to provide for clothes, furniture and other necessities. Any interruption in wages — such as layoff or inability by the breadwinner to get work — would have plunged the family into dire poverty. Similarly any heavy drinking could cause great hardship. Drink offered an escape from tenement life and alcoholism was a major problem. The custom of paying wages in pubs made this problem worse.

There were about 90,000 adult males in Dublin according to the 1911 census. About 10,000 of those were apprenticed to trades. Apart from these, a large number of labourers swelled by immigrants from rural Ireland competed for what were classified as unskilled jobs. With unemployment high, wages were low. There were approximately 25,000 'unskilled' male labourers in Dublin in 1911, paid on average less than £1 per week. For women the position was even worse. In Jacobs' biscuit factory, the city's biggest employer of women, the wages were between 35p and 37p per week. Apart from domestic service there were few jobs available for women, so their earnings added little to the family income.

TRADE UNION ACTION

The years before the First World War saw a great increase in trade union activity. Although the great Dublin Lock-out of 1913 stands out in most people's minds, there had been a number of smaller disputes from 1909. The main participants in these disputes were transport workers, who were to a great extent newly-organised into trade unions. Although many attempts had been made since 1889 to build a lasting mass organisation of unskilled workers, the first union to maintain an organisation in the face of the

above: Pay day for the children of the Industrial Revolution.

right: One of the chief aims of the early trade union movement was to reduce the number of working hours per day, which often stretched to twelve hours and over. The inscription on this commemorative watch proclaims the right to: 8 hours work, 8 hours rest, 8 hours education/leisure.

employers' counter attacks was the Irish Transport and General Workers' Union. The shape of the ITGWU was strongly influenced by two outstanding leaders, James Larkin and James Connolly.

Questions

1. Finish the sentences:
   - (a) The population of Dublin in 1901 was . . . . .
   - (b) The average wage for a tenement dweller was . . . . .
   - (c) The death rate in Dublin was higher than that of . . . . .
   - (d) Wages for women in Jacobs' were . . . . .

2. (a) Describe a typical tenement house in Dublin in 1913.
   - (b) Why did so many babies die before they reached the age of one year?
   - (c) What was the most widespread killer disease and why was it common?
   - (d) Why were drunkenness and prostitution so common in Dublin?
   - (e) List the things that the average family spent its money on.
   - (f) Why did the high level of unemployment keep wages for unskilled workers so low?

3. Explain the term 'unfit for human habitation'. Describe what a house would be like that is unfit for humans.

4. (a) What is the average wage of an industrial worker now?
   - (b) Make a list of the different things an average family would have to spend this on and say how much each item — food, clothes, etc. — would cost per week.
   - (c) Work out the weekly budget of such a family.

Discussion

Read *Alone* by Willie Birmingham. Many old people still live in conditions which are 'unfit for human habitation'. Is this right? What should be done about it?

4 · Jim Larkin and the ITGWU

EARLY DAYS IN LIVERPOOL

James Larkin was born in Liverpool in 1876. His parents were very poor Irish emigrants and he received little education before starting work at the age of eleven. However, his parents taught him a lot about Ireland and he developed a strong interest in Irish affairs. From the poverty and hardship he saw around him in Liverpool he also became a firm believer in socialism and trade unionism and he was to spend his life working for these ideas.

Larkin was tall and strong with a loud voice and a fiery temper. He had great energy and could throw himself completely into his work, giving all his time to it. Perhaps his greatest skill was as a public speaker; he spoke with such passion and sincerity that huge crowds came to hear him and were roused to action by his words. 'Big Jim', as he was usually called, was a natural leader. He soon became famous for his work for the poor of Liverpool and in 1906 he was made a paid organiser for the National Union of Dockworkers. His boss in the union, James Sexton, said that Larkin made an impact in his new job like 'the devastating roar of a volcano exploding'.

LARKIN IN BELFAST

In 1907 Larkin was sent to Belfast to organise the dockers there. He was soon involved in a major strike when the Belfast Steamship Company tried to bring 'blackleg' labour (strike-breakers) from England to replace their own workers. Larkin was arrested for attacking one of these blacklegs with a stone but when it was proved that the man had first stabbed three dockworkers and had then tried to do the same to Larkin, he was found not guilty.

As the Belfast dispute dragged on, Larkin proved his ability to persuade people to join him and encouraged the workers to keep struggling no matter what the odds against them. The carters and the city coalmen were both persuaded to come out in sympathy with the dockers and when the police were sent to break up the pickets, Larkin convinced them that they were badly paid and they also went on strike! Soldiers had to be called in to take over and many of the police were sent away to the most remote parts of Ireland.

Jim Larkin, 1914. Note the red hand badge on his lapel — the badge of the
Transport Union at the time.

ORANGE AND GREEN TOGETHER

The most amazing example of Larkin's ability to lead people and unite them behind him is the way in which he got Catholic and Protestant workers in Belfast to co-operate with and support each other. The employers cleverly tried to destroy the Belfast strike by pointing out to the Protestant workers that they were being led by a Catholic, Larkin. This type of tactic had always worked in the past but Larkin fought back with a poster which said 'not as Catholics or Protestants, as Nationalists or Unionists, but as Belfastmen and workers, stand together and don't be misled by the employers' game of dividing Catholic and Protestant'. The Protestant workers remained loyal to Larkin, saying, 'men of all creeds were determined to stand together in fighting the common enemy, the employer who denied the right of the workers to a fair wage'. In the end the Belfast strike was a success and James Larkin's name as a great leader and organiser became famous throughout Ireland.

LARKIN MOVES TO DUBLIN

In the next few years Larkin put all his energy into extending the Dockers' Union in Dublin and all around Ireland. A series of strikes followed, most of which, like the one in Cork in 1908, ended with the employers agreeing to pay the rises claimed by the men. As a result membership of the Docker's Union increased; by 1908 there were 2,800 men in the Dublin branch alone. To the employers, Larkin's energy and ability was a steadily increasing menace, and they came to hate him as much as his own followers loved him.

The Dockers' Union which Larkin was so successfully organising in Ireland was an English-based union, and the leaders of it thought Larkin was starting too many strikes which had to be paid for by the British members — there was not enough money in the Irish branches for strike pay, and Larkin had to call on the English branches for help. As a result Larkin was suspended from his job as Irish organiser and he at once left the union and set up his own, the Irish Transport and General Workers' Union.

THE GROWTH OF THE ITGWU

In the early years progress was slow for the new union, because employers were unwilling to recognise the right of their workers to belong to the new union and because of opposition from some existing unions. The first few strikes in which the ITGWU was involved were not successful. After one of them Larkin was sent to prison for a year, but he was released after three months due to petitions and demonstrations.

Gradually, due to Larkin's determination and the organising ability of his deputy, William O'Brien, the ITGWU became the leading trade union in Ireland. 1911 was the year when the union began to be successful in running strikes; that year there was a wave of strikes all over Britain and Ireland, and Larkin led the carters, the dockers, and the railwaymen in a series of disputes which gained them not only better wages and conditions, but also forced some of the employers to agree to their workers being members of a union. In 1912, Larkin organised the labourers in Dublin port and forced the management to stop casual hiring every day and to provide permanent employment. He also organised the farm labourers in County Dublin and got them a wage increase. As a result of his outstanding leadership and success in getting wage rises, workers joined the union in large numbers and membership grew from 4,000 in 1911 to 10,000 by 1913. As Larkin's success continued the employers became more and more concerned, and still hoped to stop the spread of trade unionism.

WILLIAM MARTIN MURPHY

The great success of Larkin and the growth of the ITGWU alarmed the employers and aroused them to action. The most determined of the employers and the man who quickly became their leader was William Martin Murphy, a very successful businessman who had built up a fortune in the transport business. He had built railways and tramways in Dublin, Belfast, Cork, Scotland and West Africa; he owned the *Irish Independent* newspaper, Eason's bookshop and an hotel, and had been a member of parliament.

He was very much against the tactic which Larkin and Connolly had been using since 1911, the sympathetic strike. This meant that where one group of workers was on strike another group would come out in sympathy. For example, in Cork in 1910 when the dockers went on strike, 1,000 railwaymen also came out in sympathy. This tactic had been developed by Connolly, who said that every worker, no matter which union he was in, should think of himself as a member of 'one big union' and be willing to support a strike by any other group of workers. Employers such as William Martin Murphy feared the effect the sympathetic strike would have on their business. The involvement of other groups of workers, in particular transport workers, often made it impossible to keep a factory open even if blackleg labour was available, because supplies of raw material etc. could not be brought in.

To resist this type of strike action, Murphy organised the employers of Dublin into a union of their own called the Dublin Employers' Federation. Each member company promised to work together for 'mutual protection' and to resist the use of the sympathetic strike as a weapon against any member firm. James Larkin knew that Murphy was his toughest opponent among the

5 · The Great Dublin Lock-out

MURPHY v. LARKIN

During 1913 the Dublin United Tramway Company, owned by William Martin Murphy, began sacking members of the ITGWU, Larkin's union, and replacing them with non-union labour. On several occasions, Murphy called his workers together and told them what would happen if they did not leave the union. On 19 July, he told them that if they went on strike the owners of the company would 'have three meals a day whether the men succeeded or not. I don't know if the men who go out can count on this!' Still the men refused to leave the union and in August the employers, led by Murphy, decided to smash the ITGWU once and for all. Murphy told all his workers that they must sign a promise to be loyal to their company, not to go on strike and to leave the ITGWU at once. If they refused to sign they would be sacked.

Larkin believed that if he could defeat Murphy, the opposition of the Dublin employers to the union would be defeated, but if he lost, the union could be smashed. A major clash was now only a matter of time. On 21 August 1913 two hundred tramway workers who had refused to leave the union were sacked. Larkin waited until 26 August, when the Dublin Horse Show was about to begin, before striking back. At half-past nine on that morning seven hundred employees of the Tramway Company walked off their trams leaving them wherever they happened to be. Larkin also hit at Murphy by blacking the *Irish Independent*, and calling on dockers to refuse to handle 'tainted' goods bound for Eason's and other Murphy companies.

THE TACTIC OF STARVATION

The response of the employers and the police was swift. Murphy called a meeting of the Employers' Federation and demanded that the members should lock out all employees who were members of any union, not just the ITGWU, unless they would sign a promise that they would no longer be involved in a union. This was an all-out attempt to wreck the entire trade union movement, and an inquiry later held by the government into the lock-

MR. JAMES LARKIN, DISGUISED IN FALSE BEARD AND FROCK COAT, ARRESTED
BY POLICE IN CONNECTION WITH DUBLIN STRIKE RIOTS.

above: The first food-ship arrived from Britain on Saturday, 28
September 1913.

below: Account in the *Daily Mirror* of Jim Larkin's arrest at the
Imperial Hotel, O'Connell Street.

out reported that this promise was one 'which no workman or body of workmen could reasonably be expected to accept'. On 28 August warrants were issued for the arrest of Larkin and two other leaders of the union, William O'Brien and P. T. Daly, and a meeting planned for O'Connell Street on 31 August was banned by the police. The tactics of the employers, as Murphy admitted, were to destroy the unions by starving the workers into going back. However as Keir Hardie, a Scottish socialist leader, said when speaking at a meeting in Dublin, this could take a long time because 'most of you have served too long an apprenticeship to starvation to be much afraid of that'.

THE O'CONNELL STREET RIOTS

Despite the police ban, Larkin was determined to hold the workers' meeting planned for O'Connell Street. He said:

> I am going into O'Connell Street on Sunday. I am going there alive or dead and I depend on you to carry me out if I am dead ... Remember the old song about the meeting by the river, with pikes on your shoulders by the rising of the moon. I would ask you to meet me at the old spot in O'Connell Street ...

Larkin spent the Saturday night hiding in the house of Countess Markievicz and on the Sunday morning set off for O'Connell Street disguised as an old man and wearing a false beard. Despite the ban a huge crowd had gathered, surrounded by a large force of policemen, all wondering if Larkin would be able to keep his promise and show up. Larkin stepped through the crowd and into the Imperial Hotel (now Clery's) which was owned by William Martin Murphy, and

> at half-past one precisely a window on the hotel's first floor was thrown open and out upon the balcony there stepped an imposing figure in a frock coat, an immaculate high silk hat, and a false black beard. It paused, it gazed dramatically upon the crowd: the crowd stared back. This singular apparition — it couldn't be — but it was — it was Jim Larkin! A great roar of mingled delight and laughter travelled the length of O'Connell Street. Larkin stepped forward. 'I'm here today', he boomed, 'in accordance with my promise to address you in O'Connell Street and I won't leave until I am arrested.'

He was arrested after less than a minute, but his appearance had infuriated the police, who drew their batons and launched a fierce attack on the crowd. The police batoned anyone they could catch; one person was killed and about 450 were injured on what afterwards became known as Bloody Sunday. Dublin was by now in a state of high tension. Hundreds of strikers had been arrested and the lock-out by the employers of union members was spreading every day. On 30 August, Jacobs' locked out their workers and a few days later all the coal-sellers did the same. Murphy demanded that all companies should join in and create a general lock-out all over the city. Over 400 employers agreed, and by early September over 25,000 workers were locked out of work.

THE IRISH CITIZEN ARMY

The locked-out workers gained support from many groups. Most of the leading Irish artists and writers of the day were behind the workers, including Padraic Pearse, W.B. Yeats, James Stephens, Thomas MacDonagh and George Russell. Pearse said of anyone who knew about the conditions in which the Dublin working-class lived: 'can you wonder that protest at last is made?'. Russell wrote a famous 'open letter to the Masters of Dublin' in which he said to the employers:

> You may succeed in your policy and ensure your own damnation by your victory. The men whose manhood you have broken will loathe you, and will always be brooding and scheming to strike a fresh blow. The children will be taught to curse you. The infant being moulded in the womb will have breathed into its starvation body the vitality of hate.

However, the employers refused to budge and would not listen to any talk of a deal with the unions. Violence became more a part of everyday life in the city as clashes took place between strike-breaking workers (scabs), protected by the police, and union pickets. Police assaults on workers led to the idea of forming a self-defence force to protect picketers; this is how the Irish Citizen Army came into being.

The Citizen Army was organised by Captain Jack White, an Ulster Protestant whose father was a general in the English army. He was supported by James Connolly, who had taken over the leadership of the dispute when Larkin was arrested, and by the playwright Sean O'Casey who did much of the organising. Another supporter was the Countess Markievicz. The Citizen Army quickly grew to about five hundred members and had its own flag, the Plough and the Stars. The men were drilled by Captain White, using hurleys instead of rifles, and although the lock-out was over before they had a chance to show what they could do, some of them later went on to fight under Connolly in the 1916 Rising.

AID FOR THE WORKERS

As the struggle dragged on into its second month, hardship and starvation increased among the strikers and their families. The unions had little money for strike pay and there was no social welfare system for the people to fall back on. Workers had to pawn what little they had to try to survive and to beg on the streets. The British trade unions started a fund to raise money and supplies for the Dublin workers and the response from the working people in England, Scotland and Wales was fantastic. Over £100,000 was raised and food-ships began to arrive in Dublin port, the first being the *Hare* on 28 September. Food kitchens were set up in Liberty Hall, the headquarters of the ITGWU, and food parcels were distributed to the worst-off families. Some English families offered to give a home to the children of the Irish workers until the dispute was over, but the children were stopped from leaving by the Catholic Archbishop of Dublin who feared that the families taking the children might not be 'Catholics, or indeed persons of any faith at all'.

END OF THE STRUGGLE

Although the British trade unions provided a great deal of money and food, Larkin and James Connolly wanted them to go much further. They wanted British workers to go out on sympathetic strikes and to black goods from Dublin at British ports. The British unions, however, were not willing to go this far. The money began to run out, and the union could give little help to the starving workers. The drift back to work began.

On 18 January 1914, the ITGWU leaders advised their members to return to work wherever they could, without signing the anti-union pledge if they could avoid it. Many were able to do so.

A DRAW NOT A DEFEAT

Connolly and Larkin were very bitter about the outcome of the lock-out. Connolly wrote:

> And so we Irish workers must again go down into hell, bow our backs to the lash of the slave drivers, let our hearts be seared by the iron of his hatred and instead of the sacramental wafer of brotherhood and common sacrifice eat the dust of defeat and betrayal.

Larkin publicly admitted on 30 January 1914 that the union had been defeated. Shortly after, he left for America where he was to remain for ten years.

This assessment of the lock-out turned out to be wrong. Connolly was right sometime later when he wrote 'The battle was a drawn battle'. By the summer of 1914, it was clear that the employers had failed in their objective — the destruction of Dublin trade unionism in general and of the ITGWU in particular. Trade union organisation had been destroyed in many firms but the unions themselves remained intact. In the long run the employers found it impossible to carry on their businesses without men and women who remained loyal to their union. Never again did the employers make such an effort to destroy trade unionism or to deny the right of membership to their employees. In 1914 the ITGWU was re-organised and in the following years it recovered from the lock-out and grew in strength and size.

Questions

1. (a) What did the employers hope to gain by locking out the workers?
   (b) What promise did the employers demand from the workers?
   (c) Keir Hardie said to the workers: 'you have served a long apprenticeship to starvation'. What did he mean?
   (d) Describe Larkin's appearance on the balcony of the Imperial Hotel.
   (e) Why did the police baton the people in O'Connell Street on 31 August?
   (f) Why was the Irish Citizen Army set up?
   (g) Name some of the artists and writers who supported the workers.
   (h) What help did the British labour movement give their Irish comrades?
   (i) Why did the workers begin to drift back to work?

2. Finish the following sentences:
   (a) The employers were led by .....
   (b) The workers were led by .....
   (c) The events in Dublin in 1913 are called the lock-out because .....
   (d) Before the meeting in O'Connell Street Larkin stayed with Countess .....
   (e) The organiser of the Citizen Army was Captain .....

3. Larkin and Connolly thought that the unions had been beaten. Were they right? What was the outcome of the lock-out in the longer term? Could this be done today? What sources of income do people on strike have to fall back on today?

4. Has anyone in your family ever been on strike? Ask them about it and write an account of what it was like.

Discussion

Your employer does not want his workers in a union. He offers them money to leave and says that those who do not do so will be let go. Some workers agree, others do not. Discuss and debate the views of the two groups.

a new approach to creating a revolution, called 'syndicalism'. This meant that workers, organised on the basis of the industries in which they worked rather than on their trade or job, could by supporting each other and helping each other in strikes eventually take over and operate successfully the industries in which they worked. A form of this co-operation, where all workers were to see themselves as 'one big union', was to be used by Larkin and Connolly in Ireland.

RETURN TO IRELAND

Connolly returned to Ireland in 1910, and his two books, *Labour in Irish History* and *Labour, Nationality and Religion*, were published that year. These books made him an important leader in the labour movement and he was given a job by Jim Larkin in the ITGWU as organiser in Belfast, where he was soon involved in strikes by the dockers and the women workers in the mills. In 1912, at the Trade Union Congress in Clonmel, he and Larkin proposed the setting up of the Irish Labour Party, and he was active in organising it in its early years.

CONNOLLY AND THE 1913 LOCK-OUT

Connolly played a leading role in the lock-out of 1913. He was arrested for encouraging the strikers and when he refused to take bail he was given three months in jail. He went on hunger strike at once and after eight days he was released. He spent a good deal of the lock-out period in England speaking at meetings to raise funds and trying to get the British unions to help the Dublin workers by refusing to handle goods coming from or going to Ireland. Although he considered that the lock-out ended in a draw, Connolly was very bitter about the impact of the lock-out on workers and their families. He turned his interest to the question of Irish independence. He was convinced that without independence a social revolution was impossible. He also began to think that only an armed revolt against the government could bring about independence. Shortly after the lock-out Connolly made contact with the leaders of the Irish Republican Brotherhood, who were planning a rising against Britain.

CONNOLLY AND POLITICAL REVOLUTION

When World War I broke out Connolly, who was now General Secretary of the ITGWU, placed a banner outside Liberty Hall, the union headquarters, which said 'We serve neither King nor Kaiser but Ireland'. In private he urged the IRB leaders not to let the chance for a rising slip by. In his paper, the *Irish Worker*, he called on Irishmen not to fight for Britain in World War I and urged them instead to join the Irish Volunteers or the Citizen Army.

Connolly's paper was shut down by the government but under another name he re-opened and challenged the authorities: 'If you strike at, imprison, or kill us, out of our prisons or graves we will evoke a spirit that will thwart you, and perhaps raise a force that will destroy you. We defy you! Do your worst!'

At this time Connolly published *The Re-Conquest of Ireland* in which he argued that a revolution which set Ireland free from Britain would be pointless unless there was also a change in the ownership of property from the small wealthy capitalist class to the mass of the people. He argued that: 'The conquest of Ireland has meant the social and political servitude of the Irish masses, and therefore the re-conquest of Ireland must mean the social as well as the political independence from servitude of every man, woman and child in Ireland'.

CITIZEN ARMY

During 1915 the planning for a rising went ahead and Connolly was more and more anxious for action. He decided to rebuild what remained of the Irish Citizen Army (which had been set up at the time of the lock-out to defend the striking workers from the police). He made clear the role he saw for his small workers' army: 'The Irish Citizen Army in its constitution pledges its members to fight for a Republic. Its members are, therefore, among those who believe that at the call of duty they may have to lay down their lives for Ireland ...'

Connolly grew upset at the delay in starting the rising and tried to put pressure on the IRB leaders by threatening that the Citizen Army would go it alone. Eventually the IRB leaders agreed a date. In the final weeks before the rising, Connolly prepared the two hundred men of the Citizen Army. He warned them that 'the odds are a thousand to one against us. If we win we will be great heroes; but if we lose we will be the greatest scoundrels the country ever produced. In the event of victory hold on to your rifles as those with whom we are fighting may stop before our goal is reached. We are out for economic as well as political freedom'.

In his last article before the rising he gave his reason for taking part: 'The cause of Labour is the cause of Ireland, the cause of Ireland is the cause of Labour. They cannot be dissevered. Ireland seeks freedom. Labour seeks that an Ireland free should be the sole Mistress of her own destiny'. Other trade union leaders and socialists such as Larkin and the playwright Sean O'Casey disagreed with Connolly's analysis of the situation. They also disagreed with

Connolly's decision to involve the Citizen Army in what they considered to be a purely nationalist cause which did not even have the possibility of succeeding.

THE RISING

On the morning of Easter Monday, 1916, the Military Council of the IRB meeting at Liberty Hall decided, despite the capture of the vital guns arriving from Germany in the *Aud,* to go ahead with the rising. Connolly argued strongly that they should go ahead and when the decision was made he sent for three printers and got them to print the Proclamation of the Republic on the printing machine of the ITGWU. As he went out to lead the Citizen Army into battle he said to William O'Brien, 'We are going out to be slaughtered'. 'Is there no chance of success?' said O'Brien. 'None whatever', replied Connolly. The column of about one hundred and fifty men, with Connolly and Pearse at the front, then marched up Abbey Street and occupied the General Post Office.

Connolly commanded the men fighting in the GPO throughout the week. He was described by Pearse as the 'guiding brain of our resistance' and although wounded twice, the second time badly in the leg, he refused to leave until the Volunteers were forced to surrender on Saturday, 27 April.

On Tuesday, 9 May, Connolly was tried by court martial. His trial took place at his bedside and he was sentenced to death. There was hope that because he was so badly wounded the sentence would not be carried out, but on 12 May he was taken to the prison yard in Kilmainham jail and shot, seated in a chair, by a firing squad.

A GREAT PATRIOT

James Connolly was a great leader. He described his three great loves as socialism, trade unionism and Irish nationalism. He said: 'Ireland without her people is nothing to me and the man who is bubbling over with love and enthusiasm for "Ireland" and yet can pass unmoved through our streets and witness all the wrong and suffering, the shame and degradation wrought upon the people of Ireland, wrought by Irishmen on Irishmen and women, without burning to end it, is in my opinion a fraud and a liar in his heart'. Today some, while acknowledging the enormous contribution made by Connolly to socialism and trade unionism up to and including 1913, question his decision to turn to physical force to achieve his aim and the wisdom of leading the Citizen Army into the 1916 Rising.

Connolly's life was given to the cause of the worker. He fought for the working class as a trade union organiser, as a writer and as a speaker. Finally, as he saw it, he took part in the 1916 Rising not to achieve simply Irish independence, but a Workers' Republic where the workers would own the wealth of the country.

Questions

1. (a) Where was James Connolly born?
   (b) What link did his family have with Ireland?
   (c) Why did Connolly first come to Ireland?
   (d) When Connolly returned to Ireland in 1910, what did he work at?
   (e) Name two of James Connolly's books.
   (f) What part did Connolly play in the 1913 lock-out?
   (g) Which army did Connolly lead in the 1916 Rising?
   (h) Six other men signed the Proclamation of Independence with Connolly. Name them.
   (i) How did James Connolly die?

2. Complete some of Connolly's famous slogans:
   (a) We serve neither . . . . .
   (b) The cause of labour is the cause . . . . .
   (c) If we win we will be great heroes . . . . .
   (d) Ireland without her people . . . . .

3. Connolly said his three great loves were: (1) socialism, (2) trade unionism, (3) Irish nationalism. What do you think each of these terms means?

4. Connolly's views were formed partly by the terrible working conditions he saw in his youth in Edinburgh. Read his description again. Do these conditions still exist? List some of the changes that have taken place since.

5. Connolly believed in all workers acting together as if they were in 'one big union'. What did he mean by this?

Discussion

'We are out for economic as well as political freedom,' said James Connolly before the 1916 Rising. What did he mean? If he came back to Ireland today, would he think that 'economic freedom' had been achieved by the Irish people?

fifteen years. These changes, together with free transport on special buses in country areas, a new building and repair programme and a free book scheme, have meant that for the first time secondary education is within the reach of the children of most working-class people.

THIRD-LEVEL EDUCATION

The numbers of children from working-class homes getting into a university or third-level education college, like the number who used to get into secondary school, is very small. In recent years, there has been a big increase in the number of places in third-level colleges, particularly technical colleges such as the NIHEs in Dublin and Limerick and Regional Technical Colleges around the country. However, fees are high and although a system of grants for the less well-off has existed for years, very few people of working-class background are getting a third-level education. The trade unions have been arguing for a change in educational policies and structures to rectify this unjust situation.

Conclusion

Irish living and working conditions have been improving considerably in the past fifty years, although most of the real changes have come only in the past twenty years. People are now more urbanised than they were, more likely to work in industry than on a farm and more likely to have some degree of prosperity than their grandparents or parents. However, this prosperity has not been evenly spread. As we saw earlier, 30 percent of the people depend on some form of social welfare benefit, and recent surveys show that 20-25 percent of the people still live in poverty or near poverty. Due to better social welfare, health care and housing, the poverty of today may not be as great as it was in the days of the 1913 lock-out. But with so much more wealth in the country, it is unnecessary and wrong that anyone should have to live in poverty.

The trade union movement can take much of the credit for the improvements that have occurred, especially in wages and conditions of employment, but they continue to press for major changes in economic and social policies in order to create an equal and just society.

Questions

1. Finish the sentences:
   (a) The Irish population decline stopped because . . . . .
   (b) Today half of the people are under age . . . . .
   (c) Today only one person out of every five works in . . . . .
   (d) Fianna Fail introduced the . . . . . Act in 1934.
   (e) It is said that 1,000,000 people depend on . . . . . for a living.
   (f) Free secondary education was introduced in . . . .

2. (a) The trade unions fight for better wages and conditions for their members. What other role do they have?
   (b) Why is the Irish population today so young? What problems does a young population create?
   (c) List some of the improvements in working conditions since the 1920s.
   (d) In what year were children's allowances first brought in?
   (e) What new types of social welfare benefits were introduced in the 1970s?
   (f) Who brought in free secondary school education?
   (g) When did the programme of slum clearance begin?
   (h) Why is the medical card and choice-of-doctor scheme better than the old system of visiting the dispensary?

3. Describe how Dr Noel Browne beat the dreaded disease tuberculosis. What happened to Dr Browne's other idea, the Mother and Child scheme?

4. Only a tiny fraction of working-class children go to college. Why do you think this is so? What steps could be taken to change the situation?

Discussion

(a) In England many of the tower blocks of flats built during the 1960s are now being knocked down. What are the problems of living in high-rise flats? Can you think of any other use for these flats?

(b) Explain the term 'means test'. In the past most benefits were only given after a strict means test and today also some benefits like Home Assistance require a means test. Some people say a means test is humiliating. Do you think it is? Why? What things are taken into account in a means test?

8 · Trade Union Growth 1914-1960

The ten years after the 1913 lock-out saw the trade union movement slowly recover and go on to grow steadily in numbers and power. These were years when political problems, in particular the pre-occupation with the struggle for independence, played an important role in trade union affairs.

THE STRUGGLE FOR IRISH INDEPENDENCE

When the War of Independence started in 1919, the trade union movement found itself in a difficult situation. Some members were in favour of the demand for an Irish Republic, but since the movement took in all Ireland there were in Ulster many members who were Unionists. The movement was anxious to remain unified and was very careful to stay neutral, as a resolution passed at the 1916 Conference shows. Members were asked to stand in silence, 'for all who had died for what they believed to be the cause of Liberty and Democracy and for love of their country'. This covered not only those killed in the Rising but also those who fought in the British Army in World War I.

However, despite efforts to stay out of the political struggle it was only a matter of time before parts of the movement were forced into taking political action. In the 1918 election the Irish Labour Party, which had close links with the trade union movement, did not put up candidates, in order to allow Sinn Féin a clear run. Many historians consider that in the long run this did a lot of damage to the Labour Party by putting it outside one of the main issues in Irish politics, 'the National Question'. Partly as a result of its decision in 1918, it has since remained a minority party with a small share of the seats in the Dail.

Even though sections of the Irish trade union movement gave strong support to the struggle to achieve an independent Ireland, the new state showed little sympathy for the social policies of the movement. This was partly because the division of Ireland and the relationship between Britain and Ireland continued to be the main issues in politics, and very little time was given for debate on social issues such as jobs, housing, education, health and so on. The governments of the early years of the state were also very traditional in outlook, and made very little effort to bring about social change.

50

YEARS OF GROWTH

The early years of the Republic saw a rapid growth in trade union membership. In 1914 there were 110,000 members in the various unions in Ireland, but by 1922 this had gone up to 300,000 and the ITGWU alone had more than 130,000 members. Further growth was held back by a series of internal rows which badly split the movement during the 1920s and 1930s. The first centred around a split between Jim Larkin, back from America, and William O'Brien, who had replaced him as leader of the ITGWU. The result was a new union, The Workers' Union of Ireland, and the row between the unions was to be bitter and long-lasting.

MANY NEW UNIONS

Another blow to the strength of the movement came during the 1930s when many new unions were set up, so that in most jobs there were several unions representing the workers. The large number of unions caused rivalry and division between groups of workers and sometimes led to strikes. A number of efforts was made to reduce the number of unions by getting some to join together so that there would be only one union for the building industry, one for the transport industry and so on. However, little progress was made since smaller unions did not wish to be taken over by larger ones and most of the members of the smaller unions usually voted to remain in their own union.

ANOTHER SPLIT

During the war years another, more serious, split in the movement took place, caused by a row between unions which were Irish, such as the ITGWU, and those which were English-based but had Irish members. In 1943 the British Trade Union Congress invited Irish representatives to attend a meeting of the World Trade Union Congress in London. The leaders of the Irish Congress did not want to go because the Republic was neutral in the war and they were afraid that going would damage this position. However, in 1944 the Annual Conference of the Irish Trade Union Congress decided to send delegates and as a result the ITGWU left Congress and set up its own Congress of Irish Unions. By the end of the war the labour movement was completely split.

The 1940s and 1950s were decades of little or no economic growth. Emigration remained very high, there was little new employment created, and the trade union movement did not grow a great deal. In 1947 a Fianna Fail minister, Sean Lemass, set up the Labour Court for the purpose of settling disputes between employers and employees.

above: Part of the campaign against mass unemployment in the 1950s - Dublin unemployed stage a protest march.

below: In the 1950s the main source of new jobs at home was in the expanding State companies such as the ESB, the Sugar Company and Bord na Móna.

Jim Larkin, one of the great figures of the Irish labour movement, died in 1947. The old divisions going back to the Larkin/O'Brien feud of the 1920s and the split between the Irish Trade Union Congress and the Congress of Irish Unions were finally settled when the Irish Congress of Trade Unions was set up in 1959. The trade union movement became united once again.

THE 1960s AND 1970s

The 1960s and 1970s were years of rapid development for the trade union movement as the Irish economy, and particularly industry, began to grow. Membership of unions expanded rapidly, particularly in the white-collar sector, and many more unions joined the Irish Congress of Trade Unions. From the mid-1960s grants given by the Industrial Development Authority began to attract many foreign companies to Ireland, and the number of people employed in factories rose quickly. Some of these firms at first tried to stop their workers being unionised, but bit by bit these companies were forced to recognise trade unions and relations between them and the trade unions have been quite good.

During the 1960s there was a series of major national strikes in key areas such as transport, construction, teaching and electricity. There was a major strike by maintenance workers and a long banking strike. These disputes were largely the result of a rapid improvement in the economy after nearly thirty years of little or no growth; workers were trying to keep wages in line with the rapidly-rising incomes of managers and the self-employed.

A NEW ROLE FOR THE TRADE UNION MOVEMENT

The early 1970s saw two major changes at national level in the work of the trade union movement. The first was the setting up of the 'All-Out Strike System' by the Irish Congress of Trade Unions in 1970. Under this system, if there is a dispute in a company involving a section of the workforce, the workers concerned can explain their problem to Congress which may give them the go-ahead to put an all-out picket on the firm. This means that other trade unionists in the firm may not pass the picket. All-out pickets are not always granted.

The second change was the introduction of National Pay Agreements in 1970. This meant that instead of each union negotiating with each employer there were national negotiations between all unions and all employers, and a pay rise for all workers was agreed on. From 1979 this system was further extended, and the government played an active part in the talks, which covered not only wages and conditions but other social and economic issues, such as job creation, taxes, social welfare and so on. These were called

Ferbane Generating Station was one of the first turf-
fired electrical stations operated by the ESB. these
stations, supplied by Bord na Móna, played an
important part in bringing electricity to rural Ireland,
which was essential for the growth of industry.

'National Understandings' and the different groups involved in the talks —
unions, employers and government — are sometimes called the 'social
partners'. After a return to local negotiations for most of the 1980s, the Irish
Congress of Trade Unions again became involved in negotiations at national
level early in 1987. After lengthy talks with the government a Programme for
National Recovery was agreed and voted on by the unions in November 1987.

THE CHALLENGE AHEAD

The changing industrial and social scene presents many new challenges to
the trade union movement as we enter the 1990s. A stronger, better organised
and more effective trade union movement is essential if workers' interests are
to be protected in the changing circumstances of high unemployment and
greater fragmentation of the labour force. Various economic developments

such as increased self-employment, more part-time and temporary work, increased use of technology and more employees working in small firms have serious implications for the trade union movement.

To fight these problems and to be ready for the future, unions must react to changes that are taking place in the economy and to the increased demands which are being made on them. For many unions this will involve looking at the possibility of closer co-operation and even amalgamation with other unions. A smaller number of strong unions would:

- strengthen the power of the movement and make it a more effective force in industrial relations

- extend trade union membership to unorganised workers

- improve participation by members in decision-making

- enable the movement to provide better service for members in areas like health and safety, research, etc.

The achievements of the past have been considerable, and the movement is now looking ahead with confidence to facing the challenges posed by a rapidly changing economy and society.

Questions

1. Finish the sentence:
   (a) By 1922 the ITGWU had grown to .....
   (b) When he returned from America Jim Larkin set up the .....
   (c) Larkin died in .....
   (d) Sean Lemass set up the ..... in 1946.

2. (a) Why did the trade union movement not take either side during the War of Independence?
   (b) Why did the Labour Party not put up candidates in the general election of 1919?
   (c) What damage did this do to the Labour Party in the long run?
   (d) What was the cause of the splits in the trade union movement in the 1920s and 1930s?
   (e) What new roles at national level did the trade unions take on in the 1960s and 1970s?
   (f) What is the title of the agreement negotiated between the ICTU and the government in 1987?

3. Explain the term 'All-Out Picket'. When did the unions introduce the idea? Do you think it is a good idea?

Discussion

Some trade unionists say that it is better for each union to talk directly with the employers of its members in order to get wage increases. Others say that a national agreement is better for their members. What points favour each side? Which unions would you say prefer local negotiations and which a national agreement? Why? What other things as well as pay are covered by a 'National Understanding'? Should trade unions have a say in these matters?

9 · The Modern Trade Union Movement

THE ROLE OF TRADE UNIONS

The role of the trade union movement is a broad one. The most important aspect of it is, without doubt, representing its members in their places of work. Besides wages and salaries, trade unions negotiate on behalf of their members on such things as health and safety, canteen facilities, hours of work, shift-work systems, bonus schemes, holidays, unfair dismissal and redundancy payments.

However, as we have seen, the trade union movement has always believed that an important part of its role is to represent the interests of working people not only in their jobs but in other areas which affect their standard of living. Examples of issues about which the movement is concerned include job creation, health, education, social welfare and so on. Congress and the unions seek to influence and advise governments on measures which concern workers and on economic and social issues. They put forward ideas and proposals to influence policy in favour of a better deal for the less well-off and the poor. Under present circumstances, Congress is particularly worried about the problem of youth unemployment and is pressing for more special measures to increase the training and work opportunities available for young school-leavers.

Nowadays the right of the movement to put forward views on a wide range of issues is accepted by government, and the trade unions are seen as one of the 'social partners'. To play their role to the full, Congress and unions are involved in many councils, committees and boards, for example:

National Economic and Social
  Council
Employer-Labour Conference
Commission on Taxation
Commission on Social Welfare
National Prices Commission
FÁS
Irish Productivity Centre

Youth Employment Agency
Employment Appeals Tribunal
Employment Equality Agency
EEC Economic and Social
  Committee
European Social Fund Advisory
  Committee

Women's Rights

The ICTU has long campaigned for equal rights for all workers, regardless of sex, race, creed or marital status, and has been particularly concerned about the treatment of female workers. Some improvements in this area have taken place as a result of both trade union pressure and laws introduced by the European Community, but many areas of discrimination still exist. Among the areas which the ICTU believes need to be covered by a charter of rights for women are: (1) equal pay for work of equal value, (2) elimination of discrimination against women in gaining promotion (in many jobs the majority of workers are women but only a tiny percentage of management are female — primary teaching is an example), (3) an end to the portrayal of women in the media in a sexist and stereotyped manner, (4) full equality of women under the Social Welfare Code and (5) the eradication of sexual harassment at work and in society.

Education

A very important part of achieving equal opportunity for everyone in society is that all children, no matter what their family circumstances, should have the chance to reach their full potential in the education system. At present, the majority of children from working-class homes do not complete secondary education up to Leaving Cert level, and only a handful reach third-level education. To change this, the ICTU argues that more money should be spent on primary education, in particular in areas which are poor and disadvantaged, and a special scheme of educational grants should be introduced to enable a larger number of working-class children to remain on to finish secondary school. To increase the opportunities of pupils who drop out of school early or who do not find the present courses suitable, new types of courses such as vocational preparation should be extended and the links between school and work strengthened. More facilities for adult education to cater for people who had to leave school without qualifications should be made available.

South Africa

The ICTU is strongly against the Apartheid System in South Africa and urges all its members and everyone else as well not to buy goods from South Africa. It also demands that the Irish government and other European governments should stop all trade with South Africa.

above: A range of journals published by various unions and some ICTU publications showing the variety of issues unions deal with — job creation, drug abuse, part-time workers, Third World issues.

below: Trade union members rehearsing a play.

Third World Development

In the ICTU policy document on Third World Development Donal Nevin, General Secretary, writes: 'the trade union movement has always seen itself as the advocate for the poor and oppressed; since the poor have no power, they only have their friends'. The Irish trade union movement sees it as the responsibility of developed countries such as Ireland to help to end poverty and injustice in the Third World. It is not enough to send food or support the work of Bob Geldof and Live Aid, good as that is. In the long run only an end to exploitation, and real development help, will solve the problem and the Irish trade union movement is campaigning for a new approach from the Irish government and the EEC.

Questions

1. (a) What are the two roles of the trade union movement?
   (b) List some of the boards and committees in which the trade union movement is involved.
   (c) How many unions are affiliated to Congress?
   (d) How many members do these unions have: (1) in the Republic, (2) in Northern Ireland?
   (e) Name the European organisation with which the ICTU is involved.
   (f) List some of the areas in which the ICTU has developed policies.

2. Explain the term 'Social Partner'. Who are the other social partners? What is the role of a social partner?

3. The ICTU demands an end to violence in Northern Ireland and increased government spending to create jobs. Do you agree? What do you think should be done to help the situation in Northern Ireland?

4. Mention the items that Congress believes should be covered by a charter of rights for women. What progress has been made in the area of women's rights so far? What else do you think needs to be done?

Discussion

Take one of the other areas of Congress policy mentioned in this chapter, for example, apartheid. Do you agree with Congress policy on this issue? What could be done by Ireland to end apartheid? What can be done by each person? Write an account of how it would feel to be a second-class citizen in your own country.

Project

Send for other policy documents such as the one on drug abuse. Write and present to the class a summary of the main points in the leaflet.

10 · Joining Up

WHAT ARE TRADE UNIONS FOR?

Trade unions are organisations formed by workers to protect their rights and interests. Through their activities they improve conditions of work and the general living standards of their members. The following are examples of what unions do:

- seek improvements in rates of pay, bonuses, overtime and hours of work

- work for healthy and safe conditions of work

- help to settle disputes which may arise in the workplace

- educate workers about their rights

- protect workers from unfair dismissal

- try and avoid redundancies and look for adequate compensation where they take place

General Unions

These unions have members from every type of industry and service. Members can be unskilled, semi-skilled or skilled. The three largest trade unions in this country, the Irish Transport and General Workers' Union, the Federated Workers' Union of Ireland and the Amalgamated Transport and General Workers' Union, are general unions. They have over 270,000 members and represent all grades of manual, clerical, administrative and professional workers.

White-collar Unions

These unions have members with professional, technical or clerical jobs, for example the INTO (Irish National Teachers' Organisation) or the AIT (Association of Inspectors of Taxes). Membership of white-collar unions has increased significantly in recent times. These unions have also become more militant in seeking redress of their grievances.

Employers' Unions

These unions are for factory, business and company owners and deal with their problems. The FUE (Federated Union of Employers) is the employers' union in the Republic of Ireland. It represents employers individually or collectively in negotiations at both local and national level.

As you can see, there is a wide variety of unions covering almost all types of work. In terms of membership levels for different areas of work, the best-organised sectors are the public service, state companies, large private companies like Guinness, Cement-Roadstone and Quinnsworth, and the banks. The least-organised would include small factories, offices, shops, restaurants and small employers generally. Workers in small companies often have worse conditions and rates of pay.

Questions

1. Complete these sentences:
   (a) Trade unions are organisations formed to . . . . .
   (b) Through their activities trade unions improve . . . . .
   (c) By joining a trade union you can get . . . . .
   (d) There are unions for all types of workers, for example . . . . .
   (e) A white-collar union has members such as . . . . .

2. List five services which unions provide for their members, then rank these in order of importance.

3. Find out from family members — parents, brothers, sisters, uncles, aunts, cousins — if they are in unions and, if so, what their unions are called.

4. What do you think each of these terms means:
   — Negotiate   — Unfair dismissal
   — Conditions of work   — Compensation
   — Workplace disputes

5. (a) There are four main types of union in Ireland. Give a brief outline of each.
   (b) Say which type of union each of these people might join:
   — Bus driver   — Painter
   — Bank official   — Shop owner
   — Carpenter   — Office cleaner
   — Doctor   — Factory owner

6. Select one of these opinions and comment on it:
   (a) 'Unions were needed years ago, but things have improved a lot since then and there isn't really a need for them now.'
   (b) 'On your own, you wouldn't have a hope of getting the results that workers organised in a trade union can get.'

Role-play/Further discussion

You are working in a fast-food restaurant. None of the workers is in a union. The management tells them that they must work on Sundays in addition to Saturdays or else they will lose their jobs. The workers decide to hold a meeting and to consider joining a trade union. Discuss/role-play this situation.

11 · Taking Part

HOW DO I JOIN A TRADE UNION?

You can become a trade union member by filling in an application form and agreeing to pay a subscription. You can usually obtain such a form from the union shop steward or local representative. S/he is the person elected by the workers to deal with union matters in the workplace. After you fill in your application form you may have to ask another trade union member to sponsor you. Your application form is then sent to your local union branch or to the trade union office. In most cases you will be issued with a union card. Sometimes you will need to produce this card as evidence of union membership, e.g. to participate in union elections. On joining, you may also receive a Rule Book which explains how your union is organised.

In some large firms, there may be more than one union. Before making up your mind about which one to join, you should find out as much as you can about each of them. In addition, if there isn't a trade union where you work, you still have the right to join one.

WILL I HAVE TO JOIN A TRADE UNION?

Most workers have the right to join a trade union if they wish and the majority of them do. About 60 percent of Irish workers are members of trade unions, one of the highest membership rates in western Europe. At present there are more than sixty unions catering for all categories of worker in the Republic of Ireland. Consequently union membership is open to practically all employees.

The right to join a trade union is protected by law and as a consequence you cannot be harassed or sacked from your employment just because you become a union member. Although it is in your interest to join a union, you are not compelled to do so except where a 'closed shop' arrangement exists. In such cases union membership is a condition of employment. This means that an agreement has been made with the employer that all workers in a particular place of employment will join a union.

There are two kinds of 'closed shop', pre-entry and post-entry. Where 'pre-entry' applies, a person applying for a job must be a member of a particular trade union before being employed. A 'post-entry' closed shop means that a person already in employment will be required to join a particular union as a result of an agreement between that union and his/her employer.

WHAT WILL IT COST ME TO JOIN A TRADE UNION?

The amount you pay to your union for membership will vary from one job to another, depending on the amount you earn and the job you do. However, the amount you pay to your union will be small when compared to the benefits and services you will get in return.

It is important to understand that unions aren't just a one-way thing, taking your money and offering you nothing back. Your union subscription helps to pay for the expenses of running a union, for example to pay the wages of full-time trade union officials and to publish information for members. Your union subscription will also help to fund special benefits for members who may be on strike or who face particular hardships.

HOW DO I KNOW THAT THE UNION I JOIN WILL DO WHAT I WANT?

Unions belong to their members. When you join you can play your part in deciding what your union should do. You will be encouraged to go along to union meetings, have your say and vote on how the union should do things and how it should be run.

6. Choose one of these opinions and suggest how a trade union member/ official might reply to it:
   (a) 'I don't agree that unions belong to their members. As I see it, when you join a union you get told what to do by the union instead of the bosses. So what's the difference?'
   (b) 'Unions are only interested in me for my money — why should I give some of it to them when I may earn so little anyway?'

Role-play/Further discussion

Two trade union officials are speaking to a group of workers from a clothing factory about joining a union. The workers have heard that conditions in other clothing factories are much better than theirs. They have a lot of questions they would like to ask about union membership. Role-play/discuss this situation.

12 · Organisation

To make trade unions work effectively for their members, certain rules, positions and organisation arrangements have developed over the years. While it is not intended to cover the organisation structure of each and every union, which can vary a lot, the following outline gives a general account of trade union organisations in Ireland.

THE UNION RULE BOOK

The basic document of each union is its Rule Book. It contains regulations stating how its affairs must be organised. Each union must lodge a set of rules with a government officer known as the Registrar of Friendly Societies. This officer examines the rules, and any proposed changes to them, to make sure

(f) The education of workers in social, industrial and political affairs.

(g) The extension of co-operative production and distribution.

(h) The establishment or carrying on, or participation, directly or indirectly in the business of printing or publishing a general newspaper or other newspapers, or of books, pamphlets or other publications, or of any other kind of undertaking, industrial or otherwise, for the purpose of furthering the interest of the Union or its members or of Trade Unionism generally.

(i) The furtherance of, or participation directly or indirectly in the work of any organisation: local, national, or international Union.

(k) The acquisition of property both real and personal for any lawful purpose or any manner by way of purchase, mortgage, lease, devise, gift or prescription and to sell, mortgage, exchange, let or otherwise dispose of such property.

(l) The entry into arrangement for federation, affiliation, union of interest to aid any similar organisation and to merge or amalgamate with any other Trade Union or Trade Unions and to transfer all or any of its property or assets to any Trade Union created by such merger or amalgamation.

(m) To negotiate with employers on behalf of its members, and to represent them both individually and collectively, and to conduct negotiations with a view to the settlement of disputes and differences between its members and their employers by collective bargaining and agreement, industrial action or otherwise.

(n) To obtain and maintain just and reasonable terms and conditions of employment for its members, and generally, to safeguard their rights and interests.

(o) To regulate the relations and settle disputes between this Union and its members, or between any member or members and other members of the Union.

Extract from the Rule Book of the Postal and Telecommunications Workers' Union (PTWU), showing the range of objectives covered by union constitutions.

that they are fair and just. In addition, each union must send the Registrar an annual financial statement which is open to inspection.

Every union member is entitled to receive a union Rule Book. Understanding the basic rules improves the level of participation in the affairs of the union.

WHAT A SHOP STEWARD/LOCAL REPRESENTATIVE DOES

In every workplace union members elect a spokesperson, someone to speak up for and act on their behalf, especially in dealings with management. This person is known as a shop steward or staff representative. The union Rule Book may outline the duties expected of a shop steward. In general a shop steward's duties include:

—recruiting new members
—collecting money for the union
—holding meetings and finding out the members' views
—dealing with complaints from workers and advising them of their rights
—seeing that union policies are carried out where possible
—making sure that agreements are kept
—passing on information to members
—meeting the management when minor problems need to be sorted out.

Where there is a large workforce there may be more than one shop steward, each dealing with a particular section. The shop steward is not usually paid for the union work s/he does. When a problem arises, the shop steward usually deals with the matter on behalf of his/her colleagues and is often able to settle things on the spot. However, if necessary, s/he will contact a full-time official for assistance.

WHAT HAPPENS AT UNION BRANCH MEETINGS?

To help their work, union members are organised into groups having something in common. Those groups are known as branches. A single workplace might form a branch. Alternatively a number of workplaces in the locality catering for the same industry or service might be organised into a single branch.

Branch Meetings

Branch meetings give members an opportunity to meet one another or discuss common problems which they may have.

All members have the right to attend branch meetings and should do so, because it is at these meetings that every member can have a say in the running of the union. All trade union matters can be discussed at branch meetings.

If you wanted to introduce a new policy or to change an existing one, you could put forward ideas about this at the branch meeting. Your recommendation would be known as a *motion* and you would need to find another member who would support it. Discussion would take place and if a majority accepted your motion, the matter would be taken a step further. By attending your branch meeting you can be kept up-to-date with union affairs. Where something isn't clear questions can be raised and clarifications given. Voting takes place at branch meetings, e.g. on a pay deal or new overtime rates. This type of vote is known as a *ballot*.

From amongst themselves, members elect a secretary, chairperson and committee to run the branch affairs. If you wish to do one of these jobs, you can put yourself forward for election. Also, from time to time, branch members may decide to set up a special committee to investigate and report on a particular problem, e.g. the level of part-time employment in local industries.

WHAT HAPPENS AT ANNUAL CONFERENCE?

Once a year all branches of the same union send representatives to a conference where they discuss and decide on union policy. These representatives are known as delegates. Each branch can put forward suggestions to annual conference. These proposals are then considered by the delegates from all the branches, who vote on them. If they are accepted they become trade union *policy*. It is then the job of the union to try and get the policies accepted by the employers or the government by means of negotiation and representations.

WHO IS THE NATIONAL EXECUTIVE?

Annual Conference elects a National Executive Committee to run the affairs of the union. Members of this committee are the highest-ranked officers of a union. The National Executive sees that the policy of the Annual Conference is carried out. It generally has the power to approve strike action after a vote has been taken by the members concerned. It appoints full-time officials and it makes sure that the affairs of the union are properly conducted.

WHAT DO FULL-TIME OFFICIALS DO?

It would not be possible for an ordinary worker to hold down a job and deal effectively with all the matters that arise in a trade union. As a result, unions employ full-time officials to carry out work on their behalf. They see to it that the policies of the union are implemented and they operate as professional negotiators on behalf of the members. These officials are paid from the money raised by members' subscriptions.

They do not have the power to accept a final offer from an employer. This must be voted on by the members themselves.

WHAT ARE TRADES COUNCILS?

Trades Councils are formed by different unions coming together in a particular town or area. Representatives from local unions make up the Council. There are about fifty Trades Councils in operation throughout Ireland, one-third of these in Northern Ireland and the remainder in the Republic.

The aim of a Trades Council is to promote the general industrial and social interests of its membership. It provides an important link between different unions in a locality. It also has a wider connection, being linked to the Irish Congress of Trade Unions.

THE WORK OF THE IRISH CONGRESS OF TRADE UNIONS (ICTU)

Almost all trade unions in Ireland are joined together in the Irish Congress of Trade Unions (ICTU). This organisation brings together their activities at a national and international level. Because it unites and includes so many unions, it has about eighty trade unions with well over 600,000 members in both the Republic and Northern Ireland. This makes the ICTU by far the biggest representative organisation in the country with, for example, more than three times as many members as the next biggest organisation, the Irish Farmer's Association.

All unions joined to the ICTU meet at an annual conference where trade union policy is decided by and for the whole trade union movement. Because of this, decisions taken at this conference carry a lot of weight.

The Conference elects an Executive Council to carry out its policy. The Executive Council holds discussions with the government on national issues such as unemployment, taxation, the 'state of the economy' and National Wage Agreements. In addition to this, the ICTU provides informational, educational, and training services to unions.

Questions

1. Complete these sentences:
   (a) A shop steward acts on behalf of .....
   (b) All union members have the right to attend .....
   (c) Once a year all union branches send representatives to .....
   (d) The highest-ranked officers in a union are members of .....
   (e) The ICTU is known as an 'umbrella-type' organisation because .....

2. (a) List five duties a shop steward carries out. Rank them in order of importance.
   (b) Select the qualities you think a shop steward should have and in each case say why:

Trustworthy	Courteous
Polite	Firm
Energetic	Hard-working
Stubborn	Quiet
Talkative	Determined
Friendly	Understanding
Honest	Reliable
Sympathetic	Practical
Punctual	Disorganised
Short-tempered	

   (c) Give an example of a problem you could bring to your shop steward. What do you think s/he might do about it?

3. (a) Why do you think unions are organised into branches?
   (b) What happens at union branch meetings?
   (c) The following is an example of a motion which might appear on a branch meeting agenda:
       'That the retirement age of workers in the engineering industry be reduced to 60 years, with retirement pensions more closely related to the average wage in industry'.
       Suggest arguments which could be made for or against this proposal.
   (d) Write a motion which you could present for discussion at a branch meeting. Outline what you would say in support of it.

4. Explain these terms as they relate to trade union affairs:
   — Ballot   — Annual conference
   — Special committee   — Final offer
   — Branch delegate   — National Executive

5. (a) Select the correct answer. Trades Councils are formed by:
   1) local traders
   2) county councillors

3) union officials

4) local union representatives

5) a national executive committee.

(b) What does a Trades Council aim to do?

(c) Is there a Trades Council in your town or city? Find out what you can about your nearest Trades Council.

6. Comment on any one of these statements:

(a) 'Most of the problems that arise in the workforce can be solved "on the factory floor" without calling in full-time officials.'

(b) 'There is no rule which says that you must play an active part in your union but, if members don't show an interest, a union can very quickly be ineffective.'

(c) 'Union leaders and full-time officials are not commanders ordering union members about.'

Role-play/Further discussion

The management of a large manufacturing firm gets together with a group of shop stewards to discuss two problems which have cropped up. One of these concerns a cut-back on overtime. The management says that the company is taking a loss due to the high levels of overtime and proposes a 50 percent reduction. The other problem has to do with security. Recently tools and materials were taken from the stores during working hours and were not returned or seen since. Role-play/discuss this situation.

13 · Disputes and Industrial Action

The main work of the trade union movement has to do with the settlement of claims and disputes, so that justice and fairness are obtained for members. Most of the work in this area is done quietly and without any great fuss or publicity. The disputes we tend to hear about are those which result in work stoppages arising from strike action by the workers or a lock-out by the employer.

Disputes can arise for a variety of reasons. We have already seen some examples of causes of disputes; we will now look more closely at the main sources of them. Before starting, it should be pointed out that many disputes are brought about by several causes rather than just one.

WHAT CAUSES DISPUTES?

Dismissal of a worker

An industrial dispute can arise where, for example, a worker has been sacked but the worker's colleagues and the individual's union feel that s/he should be given a second chance, or where they believe a less serious form of disciplinary action should be taken.

Redundancy

When workers are being laid off, a dispute may arise when the union objects to the occurrence, the scale, or the timing of the action, and if it believes it is not being listened to, a dispute may develop. Disputes may also arise over the length of notice or the amount of redundancy money being given.

Poor industrial relations

Disputes can occur when employers and workers do not get on well together on matters affecting the workplace. Negligence, poor communication or bad decision-making on the part of management may lead to a build-up of anger and frustration amongst the workforce. This can result in a dispute or form a background to a dispute over another matter. In some cases, an employer might refuse to recognise the right of a union to represent workers in general or on a particular matter.

Breach of agreements

Disputes can arise where changes are made in workplace arrangements without the agreement of the workers and their union. For example, a demarcation agreement, which states 'who does what', may be broken, promotion procedures may be disregarded or a 'closed shop' policy may not be upheld.

What is meant by Industrial Action?

Most disputes are settled by unions and employers through talks and negotiations. However, some disputes may prove difficult to settle and may involve different forms of industrial action. The term 'industrial action' is used to cover a variety of measures used by unions and workers to try to put pressure on employers for settlement of a dispute. Trade unions and employers almost always manage to find a solution without industrial action taking place. These settlements are generally not regarded as newsworthy by the media and you will be unlikely to hear anything about them. The following are forms of industrial action that workers may take:

Official Strike

When workers withdraw their labour to obtain improvements in their jobs, with the agreement of their union, this is known as an official strike. Strikes do not take place easily. It is only reluctantly that workers go on strike, to achieve what they feel is a just claim. Most unions have strict rules that ensure a strike can only be called:

1. When all other means of settling the dispute have failed.
2. When a majority of voting members have decided by means of a ballot to take such action.

While circumstances can vary considerably from one workplace to another, it should not be assumed that trade union members themselves always cause the problems which give rise to strikes.

When an official strike takes place, workers may receive 'strike pay' from their union. This money comes from a fund made up over the years by subscriptions from the union members themselves. The idea behind the strike pay procedure is to compensate workers for the loss of their own wages while on strike. However, the levels of strike pay seldom match or come near the wage levels of the workers themselves. While on strike, workers cannot claim unemployment assistance, but if their families need extra help, supplementary welfare benefit can be claimed.

Unofficial strike

This is a strike which is neither called nor agreed to by the union concerned. When a group of workers takes such unofficial action the dispute can be very difficult to settle.

All-Out Strikes

In this situation, all unions in a workplace, whether they are directly in dispute with their employer or not, withdraw their labour and refuse to work until a grievance has been sorted out. Permission for an all-out strike is sought through the ICTU in situations where one union is in dispute with an employer. The union in dispute applies to the ICTU for support from other unions to make its own strike action more effective. If the application for an

above: Ambulance drivers voting during a dispute with the Eastern Health Board.

below: Catering workers in dispute with their employers, having been granted an all-out strike by the ICTU.

Avoca miners protest the mine's closure.

all-out strike is successful then members of other unions in that employment are expected to honour the all-out picket.

Other forms of Industrial Action

—a 'sit-in': where this takes place, workers, instead of leaving their place of work, decide to occupy it and stay on the premises without working.

—a 'work-to-rule': here workers decide to limit their work duties by sticking strictly to the rules. The idea behind this form of action is to call attention to their grievance.

—a token stoppage: in order to highlight an issue, which they feel has either been ignored or has not been dealt with properly, workers may stop work for a brief period to demonstrate their concern.

—a political strike: this type of action is directed against the government rather than against a particular employer. Unions may wish to protest about overall wage policy, taxation or the government's policy on job creation. Workers may stop work for a brief period to go on a protest march or to attend a meeting.

What is a Picket?

Workers who are taking industrial action often gather at the approaches to their workplace, usually with placards, to give information about their grievance to other workers or to members of the public. This is known as a 'picket'. Workers on picket duty usually talk to people and try to persuade them not to pass the picket. Whether the strike is a single union strike or an ICTU 'all-out' strike will be shown on the placards.

Where there is a picket by a union the workers are entitled to call on other members of their union to respect the picket by not passing it. Where an all-out strike is taking place, all union members (this will involve different unions), whether directly in dispute or not, are called on to stop work and not to pass the picket. There are few exceptions to this rule, unless special permission has been given to permit certain people to perform work, e.g. some hospital workers may be allowed to perform work in order to preserve life or handle emergencies.

When an employer is faced with a strike picket outside the premises s/he may take steps to have the picketing stopped. An order to stop picketing is known as an *injunction*. There are three types of injunctions which employers can get from the courts:

Interim Injunction

Interim injunctions are granted in almost all cases where employers apply for them. They are granted for a short period (5-10 days) and without the union's case being heard.

Interlocutory Injunction

If the dispute is not settled by the time the interim injunction runs out and the employer still wants picketing stopped or restricted, s/he may apply to the High Court and seek an interlocutory injunction. At this stage the union, through its legal representatives, can make its case known to the court. An interlocutory injunction, if granted, lasts until a full court trial is held, which can be up to one year.

Perpetual or Absolute Injunction

This injunction, if granted, would last forever, or until a further different order was given. When applied for, both sides are entitled to be present and legally represented in court. If granted, the union/workers must stop picketing. The majority of industrial disputes never reach this stage, the cases having been settled before this.

A large number of cases never pass the first, interim injunction, stage. If the picketing union does not seek legal advice, or the picket is not agreed to by the union, or if the picketing workers are not members of a union, they usually give up after the interim injunction is granted, even though the law may be on their side.

WHAT HAPPENS IF AN INJUNCTION IS DISOBEYED?

It is up to an employer, not the gardai, to see that an injunction is obeyed. If an employer decided to ignore a picket which continued despite an injunction, nothing would happen. On the other hand, the employer could inform the court that the injunction was being broken. In that case, the workers involved would be summoned to appear in court and told to respect the injunction. If they failed to do so, this would be known as 'contempt of court'. If the employer complained to the court again, the court would take action. It could order the confiscation of the workers' property or it could send them to jail. If they were sent to jail, they would remain there until they apologised to the court and promised to obey the injunction in future.

Questions

1. Complete the sentences:
   (a) The most common disputes have to do with .....
   (b) Most disputes are settled by unions without .....
   (c) A demarcation agreement states .....
   (d) When workers stop work in protest for a brief period, this is known as
       .....
   (e) Permission for an all-out strike is given by .....

2. State whether each statement is true or false. If false, correct the statement:
   (a) The disputes we hear most about are the ones which are settled
       without industrial action.
   (b) Most disputes are settled by strikes.
   (c) An official strike is where union officials refuse to work.
   (d) An unofficial strike is not supported by a trade union.
   (e) A Court Order to stop picketing is known as an injunction.

3. Briefly explain each of these terms:
   — Redundancy   — Political strike
   — Promotion procedure   — Strike pay
   — Poor industrial relations   — Sit-in

4. (a) Unions do not go on strike without good cause. According to union
       rules, under what circumstances can official strikes take place?
   (b) An all-out strike in a workplace means that all unions withdraw their
       labour. Describe the stages which can lead to this.

5. When workers go on strike they usually picket the approaches to their
   workplace to:
   — show their disapproval of an employer's action
   — let the public know about their strike
   — dissuade people from entering the workplace
   — inform other workers about their grievance.
   (a) Rank these reasons 1 to 4 in order of importance.
   (b) In your opinion, which of these reasons is (1) the most important and
       (2) the least important? Say why.

6. (a) An order to stop picketing is known as an injunction. There are three
       types of injunction. Briefly explain each type.
   (b) What happens if a court injunction is disobeyed?

7. Select one of these questions and comment on it. You may agree or
   disagree with it.
   (a) 'I think there are too many strikes. They always cause disruption and
       damage to many people not connected with the dispute. The

government should pass laws and make it very difficult for workers to withdraw their labour.'

(b) 'Unions only go on strike as a last resort, when all other means have failed to settle a dispute. The freedom to go on strike is essential, otherwise the employers could do what they liked.'

(c) 'Strikes cause hardship, bad feeling and loss of money. The only way to avoid them is for governments and employers to ensure that workers are paid well and that their conditions of work are safe and healthy.'

Role-play/Further discussion

A group of laboratory technicians in a chemical firm were not granted a pay increase in line with a recent pay round. Negotiations between the technicians' union and their employer failed to obtain the increase. After holding a ballot and seeking approval from their union, the technicians went on official strike. They looked for the support of other unions in the firm and asked their union to apply for an all-out strike from the ICTU. The Industrial Relations Committee of the ICTU met to consider their application. Discuss/role-play and develop this situation.

14 · How Trade Unions Work

SETTLING DISPUTES — NEGOTIATIONS

The aim of a trade union is to protect and advance the interests of its members. In simple terms, this means that unions help you to get the things you are entitled to, and help to prevent you being deprived of your rights as a worker.

Many workers consider that the most important job of any union is to ensure that their weekly pay-packets are adequate and that their jobs are secure. In pursuing these aims, disputes can occur. A dispute takes place when an employer and a union seriously disagree about a matter such as rates of pay, hours of work, or length of holidays. The discussions involved in settling a dispute are usually referred to as the negotiations.

The proposed settlement is then put to a ballot and a small but clear majority votes to accept the offer. The union officials undertake to process a further claim after a nine-month period and the shop stewards agree to keep a close watch on the working of the agreement.

Whether pay settlements or new agreements on working conditions are worked out to cover the workplace or whole industries or at national level, they nonetheless follow this pattern of claim, negotiations and settlement.

While most disputes can be avoided or settled quickly, others may last for a considerable time. However, no dispute lasts forever and a settlement, however difficult that may be, is eventually reached. After pay negotiations, the other areas which receive most attention from unions concern job security, health and safety at work and legal changes affecting workers.

Job Security

Security of employment is vital to all members and forms a large part of the work of any union. Unions do their best to ensure that no worker is unfairly dismissed, and have been active in bringing into existence appeal bodies such as the Employment Appeals Tribunal. Where a union feels that a member has been treated unfairly, the matter may be investigated and justice sought through such channels.

Unions also try to prevent redundancies. Where they occur, they ensure that workers receive their proper entitlements such as redundancy payments. They negotiate with government and employers to increase such entitlements.

Health and Safety

Changes are sometimes introduced in the workplace which affect the health, safety and comfort of the workers. It is part of a union's job to negotiate satisfactory working conditions.

Unions can insist that employers observe the law as laid down by the Dail under various government acts, e.g. the Factories Act and the Office Premises Act. These ban certain practices, such as the use of machinery without guards, and require inspectors to visit factories from time to time.

Legal Changes

In cases where the unions consider the law doesn't go far enough, they will bring pressure to bear on the government to make changes in the relevant acts or to introduce new legislation. Unions are aware that the use of new materials and processes in industry can lead to health and safety problems, and can alert the government and employers to the need for new regulations.

92

Questions

1. Complete these sentences:
   (a) A union demand for something is called . . . . .
   (b) Discussions to settle a dispute are known as . . . . .
   (c) When talks are suspended this means that . . . . .
   (d) A concession means that . . . . .
   (e) Agreement reached after a dispute is called . . . . .

2. Explain these terms:
   — Pay bargain   — Unfair dismissal
   — Job security   — Industrial legislation
   — Redundancy   — Appeal bodies

3. (a) Laws covering health and safety at work are made by:
       (1) The law courts
       (2) Employers
       (3) Union members
       (4) The government
       (5) Union officials
   (b) What contribution do trade unions make to the introduction of new laws affecting working conditions?

4. Comment on one of these opinions. You can agree or disagree, giving reasons for your point of view:
   (a) 'Never mind about the conditions — the only really important job of my union is to see that the pay is good.'
   (b) 'In my opinion, after negotiations, unions generally end up getting less than their members want. The officials need to be more stubborn and show greater determination going into talks.'
   (c) 'It is better to negotiate and give in a bit, than to keep holding out for what may be impossible and result in deadlock.'

Role-play/Further discussion

Recently, some temporary clerical workers have been employed by a subsidiary of an American computer firm in Dublin. Their rates of pay and terms of employment are less favourable than those of the permanent staff. While they are glad to have jobs, the temporary workers are not happy for their future prospects. A manager of the firm was heard remarking that there was no such thing as a permanent job and that all jobs were really temporary. The temporary staff wish for greater security and want their conditions improved. They approach the shop stewards to see what can be done.

Role-play/discuss this situation through the stages of claim, negotiations and settlement.

15 · Disputes

THE ROLE OF THIRD PARTIES

Most industrial disputes are solved by direct negotiations between employers and unions. What happens if a settlement isn't reached in this matter?

It sometimes happens that agreement is not reached by direct negotiations, e.g. if union members decide that the employers' final pay offer to their claim is not enough. When this happens each side may begin to put pressure on the other, in order to get a settlement that suits it. The union might, for example, ban all overtime and so make it difficult for the employer to provide normal service to customers. Other forms of industrial action include a work-to-rule, one-day strikes or all-out strikes.

When negotiations between an employer and a union seriously break down the dispute can be referred to an independent body. This means that an expert, who is not involved in the dispute, is asked to make a recommendation which both sides may agree to accept.

THE ROLE OF THE LABOUR COURT

The Labour Court was set up by the government in 1946, to provide a means whereby difficult industrial disputes could be sorted out. Despite its name the Labour Court is not a court of law. Compared to the law courts, its procedures are informal. Either side, union or management, can take a case to the Labour Court. In most cases the outcome of a court investigation is a *recommendation*, which is not legally binding on the parties. This means that neither side is compelled to accept the court ruling, but in the majority of cases the parties do accept the decision.

The Labour Court consists of a chairperson, three deputy chairpersons and eight ordinary members, all of whom are appointed by the Minister for Labour. Of the eight ordinary members, four are put forward by the employers' organisations and four by the ICTU. Normally the court operates with three people, the chairperson (or deputy chairperson), an employers' representative and a union representative.

The Industrial Relations Officer

Before the court undertakes the investigation of a dispute, it appoints an Industrial Relations Officer. This person acts as a mediator (go-between) assisting both employer and union to reach an agreement. The Industrial Relations Officer will normally find it necessary to have private discussions with each side separately. Generally speaking, it is as a result of these talks that most progress is made, because in private each side is prepared to reveal its exact and true position in the knowledge that its confidence will not be abused. As a result of these discussions the Industrial Relations Officer will have a clearer picture of what might settle the dispute. From then on s/he will be able to guide the parties along certain lines. S/he may be in a position to come forward with a solution and persuade each party to the dispute to accept it.

If the dispute is not settled at this stage, it can, at the request of either side, be referred for a full investigation and recommendation to the Labour Court. This takes the form of a Labour Court hearing.

The Labour Court Hearing

Hearings are held in private unless one of the parties concerned requests a public hearing. Written submissions are normally made by both sides. The

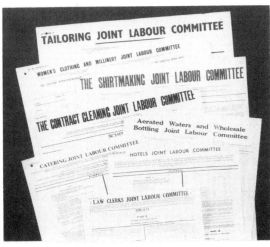

above: The Labour Court — the union side presents its case to the three members of the court while the court secretary takes notes. Following the hearing, a recommendation is issued by the court.

below: Posters for the workplace issued by the Labour Court giving the rates of pay for different industries covered by the Joint Labour Committees.

court members question both sides on their submissions. Each side is also free to question the other on its submission.

The court members consider the submissions and after about three weeks, the court makes a *recommendation* setting forth its opinion on the merits of the dispute and the terms on which it should be settled. Except in a limited number of cases, where it is agreed in advance to accept the recommendation, the court's proposals are not legally binding on the parties. However, the parties to a dispute will be expected to give serious considerations to the terms of settlement recommended by the court.

RIGHTS COMMISSIONERS

There are four Rights Commissioners appointed by the Minister for Labour. In general, their function is to deal with disputes surrounding individuals. A Rights Commissioner will investigate a trade dispute provided that:

(a) Both sides agree to the investigation;
(b) It is *not* a dispute connected with rates of pay, hours or times of work, or annual holidays of a *group* of workers;
(c) The Labour Court has not already made a recommendation about the dispute;
(d) The workers have access to the Labour Court. Workers who do not have access to the Labour Court are civil servants, teachers and some Local Authority officers: their claims on pay and conditions are dealt with by an Arbitrator who is appointed by the government.

Having investigated an individual's grievance the Rights Commissioner will make a recommendation to settle the dispute. If one party to the dispute isn't happy with the recommendation an appeal may be made to the Labour Court. The Labour Court hearing will be held in private. In such cases the parties to the dispute will be bound by the decision of the Labour Court.

EQUALITY OFFICERS

Under the provisions of the Anti-Discrimination (Pay) Act, 1974 and the Employment Equality Act, 1977, disputes concerning equal pay entitlements and discrimination in employment on grounds of sex or related to marriage may be referred to an Equality Officer of the Labour Court for investigation and recommendation. All workers are entitled to take a grievance to an Equality Officer.

During the course of an investigation, the Equality Officer examines written submissions made by the parties, meets them and may visit premises to inspect work in progress and examine records or documents.

Following this investigation, the Equality Officer issues a recommendation to the parties and to the Labour Court. Either party to the dispute may, within 42 days from the date of the recommendation, appeal to the Labour Court against it, or for an order to implement the recommendation. The court's findings in such cases are binding on the employer.

JOINT INDUSTRIAL COUNCILS

Joint Industrial Councils are negotiating bodies for particular industries or parts of industries. They are voluntary associations in which one side represents employers and the other side unions. They usually meet in the Labour Court premises and the Labour Court provides a chairperson, who is an Industrial Relations Officer, and a secretary. An example of a Joint Industrial Council is the Joint Industrial Council for the Construction Industry.

JOINT LABOUR COMMITTEES

These committees fix legal minimum rates of pay and regulate conditions of employment for certain industries, mainly industries such as agriculture, clothing and textiles, solicitor's clerks and hotels, where workers are relatively low paid. The Committees are appointed by the Labour Court and equally represent employers and unions. The chairperson is appointed by the Labour Court and the Minister for Labour may appoint other independent people to the committee.

Almost all proposals submitted by a Joint Labour Committee to the Labour Court are accepted. An Employment Regulation order is then made. The minimum rates of pay and conditions recommended by a Joint Labour Committee then become compulsory and employers are bound under penalty to pay these rates and observe the conditions. This is the nearest we have in the Republic of Ireland to a legal minimum wage, such as exists in many EEC countries.

Questions

1. Complete these sentences:
   (a) The Labour Court was set up in the year .....
   (b) A Labour Court proposal for settlement of a dispute is known as a
       .....
   (c) An Equality Officer investigates disputes about .....
   (d) Rights Commissioners are appointed by .....
   (c) Joint Labour Committees consider .....

2. State whether each statement is true or false. If false, correct the statement.
   (a) The Labour Court is a Court of Law.
   (b) Only employers can take disputes to the Labour Court.
   (c) The Labour Court normally questions both parties to a dispute.
   (d) Members of the Labour Court are appointed by the Minister for Labour.
   (e) Unions must accept all decisions of the Labour Court.
   (f) A Rights Commissioner only deals with disputes surrounding an individual worker.

3. Explain these terms:
   — Work-to-rule   — Industrial action
   — Arbitration   — Minimum wage
   — Mediator

4. (a) Why do you think the Labour Court was set up?
   (b) Describe how an Industrial Relations Officer investigates a dispute.
   (c) Outline the procedures involved in a Labour Court hearing.

5. (a) Suggest an example of the type of problem an Equality Officer deals with.
   (b) How does an Equality Officer investigate a dispute?
   (c) What happens after an Equality Officer issues a recommendation to settle a dispute?

6. Select one of these opinions and comment on it.
   (a) 'Really I don't see the need for arbitration. It takes time and costs a lot of money. Unions and employers should sort out their own problems themselves.'
   (b) 'I can't see what the point of the Labour Court is, when all of its recommendations aren't binding on both parties in a dispute.'

Role-play/Further discussion

Electrical technicians in a branch of a large Japanese firm want a 6 percent pay increase in line with wage settlements for other workers in the same sector. Their employer pleads inability to pay. After negotiations and a six-week strike fail to settle the dispute, both sides agree to go to the Labour Court. Role-play/discuss this situation.

Project

Find out the legal minimum wage as agreed by one of the Joint Labour Committees (e.g. clothing) and see if it is being paid in your area.

16 · Women

Since the growth of the factory system in the nineteenth century, increasing numbers of women have been employed in industry. A labour force survey carried out in 1985 found that 31 percent of all persons at work in the Irish Republic were women. According to this survey 57 percent of working women were single, 38 percent were married and 5 percent separated or widowed. The following table shows the employment pattern of women according to occupational groups (1985):

Occupational Category	Women as % of total
Personal services (e.g. hotel work, hairdressing)	64
Professional services (e.g. teaching, health care)	57
Insurance and Finance	47
Retail Distribution	40
Manufacturing Industry	27

When one looks more closely at the type of work women do the following picture emerges (1985):

Occupation	Women as % of total
Clerical	73
Shop assistants	57
Service workers	55
Professional and technical	49
Administrative, executive and managerial	12
Registered AnCO apprentices	0.5

These figures highlight sex segregation in the labour market. They demonstrate a form of discrimination, in that the majority of women workers are restricted to certain occupations in a limited range of employments.

Women's earnings are often considerably lower than men's. The average weekly earnings of women engaged in manufacturing industries in June 1986 was 60.5 percent of men's earnings.

THE WOMEN'S CHARTER

In seeking improvement of employment opportunities, better working conditions and more rights for women, the ICTU has drawn up a set of demands known as the Women's Charter. The ICTU, both in its dealings with government and employers, campaigns for the following policies for women:

1. The right of women to work regardless of marital status, including the right to return to work after a period of absence.

2. Equal pay for work of equal value and the introduction of a national legal minimum wage to tackle the problem of low pay.

3. Equality in conditions of employment and the elimination of all forms of direct and indirect discrimination.

4. Equal access to opportunities, promotion and work experience.

5. Full legal protection, adequate pay and benefits for part-time workers.

6. Elimination of discriminatory age-limits in the public and private sectors.

7. Equal access to all levels of education, the elimination of all forms of sexism (discrimination on grounds of sex) and a positive programme aimed at promoting equality and ensuring equal opportunities for both sexes.

101

8. Special training programmes to encourage more women into higher skilled jobs and non-traditional occupations (e.g. craft and technical jobs).

9. The working environment to be adapted to ensure the health, safety and welfare of women workers.

10. The re-organisation of working time and an overall reduction in working hours.

11. 26 weeks maternity leave on full pay, the latter 12 weeks to be taken by either parent. A minimum period of 15-20 days leave for family reasons.

12. Eradication of sexual harassment (physical and mental abuse or pressure) in all its forms.

13. Protection of women's health through the provision of a comprehensive health service on a local basis (e.g. pregnancy care and health educational services).

14. Recognition of divorce as a basic civil right. An end to the constitutional ban on divorce and the introduction of divorce legislation.

15. An end to the portrayal of women by the media in a sexist manner.

16. The provision of comprehensive childcare facilities to be provided free and controlled by the state, including after-school and holiday care facilities and school meals.

17. The elimination of all forms of direct and indirect discrimination against women in the social welfare code.

18. Provision of comprehensive contraception services, freely available and accessible to all.

19. The taking of appropriate measures to ensure that civil and criminal law protects and supports the rights of women.

The ICTU holds that it is not enough to have policies which look well on paper, but that these policies must be promoted at every level, nationally and locally. The ICTU believes that, at local level, equal opportunities in the workplace must be promoted through positive action programmes. These programmes should be based on the following principles:

— the elimination of all forms of direct and indirect discrimination

— the need to take positive steps to place women in positions they would have occupied if there had been no discrimination in the first place.

WOMEN AND THE ICTU

Special provision for women's affairs is made as follows:

1. The ICTU has two women's committees dealing specifically with trade union matters affecting women, one for the Republic and the other for Northern Ireland. They discuss such matters as low pay, equality legislation, education, training, job-sharing, child-care facilities and social welfare. Recommendations from these committees are forwarded for implementation to higher executive level.

2. Women are nominated by the Women's Committee on various committees of the ICTU, e.g. Health and Safety Committee, Education and Training Committee. Women trade unionists are also nominated to serve as ICTU representatives on outside bodies e.g. the Employment Appeals Tribunal, Employment Equality Agency.

3. As a form of positive discrimination and to ensure female participation, two seats on the Executive Council of the ICTU are reserved for women. Apart from this women may be freely elected to the other seats on the Executive Council.

4. A Women's Conference is held annually, attended by delegates from affiliated trade unions and Trades Councils.

5. The ICTU organises special training and educational courses for women trade unionists.

6. Information on issues of special concern to women workers is published.

7. Motions dealing with trade union matters affecting women are debated at the Annual Conference of the ICTU.

8. The ICTU has drawn up a document dealing with demands for employment improvements and rights for women, known as a Women's Charter. This document is kept under review and efforts are made to further the principles of it.

PARTICIPATION BY WOMEN IN TRADE UNIONS

About one-third of trade union members are women. Some unions have few or no women members, but the majority do, including some with a large female membership. While there has been some increase in the participation of women in union affairs — as shop stewards, union officials, union committee and executive council members — women are still under-represented in these areas. In a recent survey some unions stated that they

above: Delegates attending the
ICTU women's conference.

left, above and right: Women work in all types of occupations from computing to manual labour.

have carried out measures to ensure greater participation by women as follows:

1. Adoption of a positive and active policy to ensure greater participation by women.

2. Reservation of seats for women on executive councils.

3. Establishment of National Women's Committees.

4. Provision of creche facilities at Annual Conferences.

5. Appointment of Equality Officers.

6. Establishment of Women's Committees at branch/local level.

These measures indicate a willingness to encourage greater participation by women in their unions.

Questions

1. Complete these sentences:
   (a) Since the growth of the factory system in the nineteenth century increased numbers of women have . . . . .
   (b) Women in the manufacturing industry are the lowest . . . . .
   (c) The ICTU demands for employment improvements and rights for women are known as . . . . .
   (d) Sexism means . . . . .
   (e) Two seats on the Executive Council of the ICTU are . . . . .

2. Say whether each statement is true or false. If false, correct the statement:
   (a) Most working women are married.
   (b) More women than men are employed in clerical jobs.
   (c) Less than 10 percent of AnCO apprentices are female.
   (d) The ICTU campaigns for 26 weeks maternity leave on full pay.
   (e) The majority of trade unions have no women members.

3. Complete these sentences by selecting the correct answer:
   (a) The lowest rate of female employment is in: (i) retailing (ii) manufacturing (iii) insurance and finance (iv) none of these.
   (b) One-third of trade union members are: (i) unemployed (ii) women (iii) technicians (iv) none of these.
   (c) The ICTU Women's Charter demands: (i) discrimination against men (ii) a ban on divorce (iii) equal pay for equal work (iv) none of these.
   (d) The ICTU Women's Charter demands an end to: (i) sexual harassment (ii) overtime (iii) part-time work (iv) none of these.
   (e) A conference for women trade unionists is: (i) only an idea (ii) never held (iii) held annually (iv) none of these.

4. The Women's Charter
   (a) Select any ten of the demands in the Women's Charter and rank them in order of importance.
   (b) Give reasons for the ranking of your top three demands.
   (c) Is there any demand in the Women's Charter with which you don't agree? If so, give your reasons.

5. Select one of these opinions and comment on it. You may agree or disagree with the opinion stated.
   (a) 'You cannot say that you believe in equality or a fair society and then say that a woman or a married woman should not be allowed to work.'
   (b) 'Employers tell us that women have equal pay, but equal pay with whom? The average woman, because of her limited education or training has very little career opportunities and ends up in the lower-paid, mainly female section of the workplace.'
   (c) 'I think it is all right for women to work — very few families can live properly on one wage anyway — but when it comes to union activity, I think married women should put their family responsibilities first.'

Role-play/Further discussion

At the Annual Conference of a large white-collar union, delegates had before them a motion which read:

> 'That three seats on the Executive Council shall be reserved for women members, who shall be elected by separate ballot in the same manner as other members of the Executive Council.'

The supporters of this motion felt that a policy of positive discrimination was needed to encourage women to take a more active part in their union. However, some trade unionists felt that the proposal was unfair and degrading to women. They felt that the best people, men or women, should be elected to the Executive Council. Other members sympathised with the aims of the motion but felt that as a tactic the proposal wasn't correct. The media had taken particular interest in this issue and awaited the result of the debate with interest. Discuss/role-play this situation.

17 · Young People

The Irish Congress of Trade Unions supports the right of young people to participate fully in the economic, political and cultural life of the community. The most important right of all is the right to work, as without employment young people cannot be independent. But unemployment is not the only issue of concern to young people; other issues include education and training, homelessness, health care and drug abuse. Due to the efforts of the trade union movement progress has been made in certain areas, for example, with regard to the laws covering young workers, but more needs to be done. The ICTU is campaigning for the introduction of a Charter for Youth designed to improve the rights of young people and to increase the services and resources available to them. This chapter will therefore examine ICTU policy on youth, and will show how much needs to be done in the area.

YOUTH MEMBERSHIP

To improve communication between young people and trade unions, the ICTU has established Youth Committees in the Republic and in Northern Ireland. It is also very anxious to increase the participation of young people in trade unions, to take action on behalf of young workers in low-paid employment and to prevent breaches of the law concerning them. As a step towards achieving this goal, the ICTU wishes to extend the benefits of trade union membership to young people on AnCO courses, youth employment schemes and work experience programmes, as well as to those in part-time and temporary work and to those who work in small companies.

Proposals for a Youth Charter

The ICTU wishes to see a Charter for Youth introduced by the government, which would guarantee the provision of the resources necessary to meet the needs of today's young people. Among the important recommendations in the ICTU Youth Charter are:

EMPLOYMENT

1. New policies to create enough jobs for all young people.
2. A national minimum wage to protect young people from exploitation.
3. Reduction in working hours to improve employment opportunities for young people.
4. The opportunity for young workers to take part in decisions affecting their jobs and their future.

Education/Training

1. Equal access for all to education and in particular measures to increase the participation of disadvantaged youth in second and third-level education.
2. The reduction in pupil/teacher ratios through the employment of unemployed teachers.
3. The further development of imaginative alternative and additional curricula to the Leaving Certificate, and special provision of second-chance education for early school leavers and disadvantaged youth.
4. A single agency such as FÁS should have responsibility for the co-ordination and supervision of all youth schemes.
5. Young people in schools and colleges should be consulted on issues that affect them.

109

above: Singer/songwriter Paul Brady addressing the ICTU Youth Summer School (1987) on music and how it relates to young people.

below: An informal discussion with members of the ICTU Youth Committee at the Youth Summer School.

YOUNG PEOPLE AND THE LAW

1. Provision of special treatment centres for drug abusers in custody.

2. Increased efforts to rehabilitate young offenders in the community rather than in prison.

3. The age of criminal responsibility to be raised to fifteen years.

4. Removal of the status of illegitimacy.

HEALTH AND SOCIAL WELFARE

1. Young persons to be eligible for the full range of welfare and health benefits.

2. A programme of health education for all young persons, with special emphasis on prevention of drug and alcohol abuse.

Protective Legislation

1. Strict enforcement of labour legislation to prevent exploitation of young workers.

2. Improved recreation facilities for young people with access for all, including the young unemployed.

Peace and Justice

1. Removal of the threat of nuclear war by putting an end to the arms race.

2. Promotion of awareness of the problems of the Third World.

Questions

1. Give two reasons for the negative views which some young people have of trade unions.

2. There are six categories of young workers whom the ICTU wishes to recruit. Mention at least four of these.

3. List what you consider to be the five most important items in the ICTU Youth Charter.

4. Have you any proposals which you would like to have included in the Charter? Give reasons for your answer.

5. List the recreational facilities required in your locality.

6. Do you think that young people should be consulted about what goes on in their schools? How could this be done?

Young people are given the chance to express their views at ICTU
Youth Conferences.

Discussion
(a) Does the present education system reinforce existing class structures?
(b) How could the courses which you are doing at school be improved?
(c) Is the Third World our concern?
(d) Should children under fifteen years of age be treated as criminals?

112

18 · Unions and the Media

Coverage by the media (television, radio and newspapers) tends only to concentrate on a small aspect of union activities. What the public generally see or hear about are major industrial conflicts and disputes, and the routine work of unions is seldom mentioned. Sometimes coverage of disputes is sensational and the media can oversimplify what may often be very complicated situations. This chapter considers the treatment of trade unions by the media and the portrayal of and participation by women in the media.

COVERAGE OF DISPUTES

When a dispute develops between an employer and a union, our first knowledge usually comes from television, radio or a newspaper. We seldom know any of the people involved in a dispute and we depend on the media for our information. It is quite likely that many people confine their news sources to television and radio and may never read more detailed newspaper accounts.

Generally the media only begin to cover a dispute when industrial action is being threatened — this makes it newsworthy. When we hear the news on the radio or see it on television we need to remember that the reports are normally only summaries of the major relevant facts. A news item is usually confined to between one and three minutes coverage, so one cannot expect a full and detailed account of a complicated dispute in that time. Radio Telefis Eireann is obliged by legislation to present balanced news coverage. No such obligation applies to newspapers, magazines or pirate radio stations.

When people hear of a dispute resulting in industrial action, their first thought, naturally enough, is for themselves and how the dispute will affect them. Media portrayal of disputes often arouses negative reactions by emphasising the bad effects of strikes and other forms of industrial action.

WHAT MAKES THE HEADLINES

Good news is rarely as sensational as bad news and sensational stories help to sell newspapers. This has two consequences. Firstly, good news rarely features on the front page — it is more likely to be tucked away on an inside page. This means that when the media report the positive work of unions or give very full accounts of disputes, only those who read newspapers thoroughly will be aware of these facts.

Secondly, newspapers tend to use large, heavy print and emotive headlines on their front pages. A single such headline will register with many people who may not bother to read the story underneath. The following sample is typical of newspaper headlines: 'STRIKE CHAOS', 'HARDSHIP CAUSED BY STRIKERS', 'PICKET BRINGS INDUSTRIAL STANDSTILL', 'MILITANT WORKERS TO BLAME'. The net effect of these two factors — scant coverage of positive union news and emotive headlines — helps to create a negative impression of union activities in the minds of many people.

UNION VIEWPOINT

It is important to remember that no one likes to be involved in an industrial dispute. In general, workers will not embark on industrial action unless they feel very aggrieved and are convinced that no other means would resolve their dispute. Strike action is very much a last resort, taken reluctantly after much consideration. An opposite impression is often given by the media. Whenever you hear of a dispute, try to put yourself in the place of one of the workers involved in it, and where possible look beneath the surface of media reports. Many unions publish their own newsletters for their members outlining in full their current problems, and it can be very revealing to compare reports in a union newsletter with those in a national newspaper.

Front page of the *Saturday Herald* showing the media treatment of strikes on 6 September 1913.

WOMEN AND THE MEDIA

In recent years much discussion has taken place at ICTU Conferences on the treatment of women in the media, especially in advertising, and on the limited participation of women in certain areas of the media.

Women and Advertising

Two criticisms are made of the portrayal of women in advertising. Firstly, it is argued that advertisements usually project a limited image of women, confined to the traditional roles of mother and housewife, despite the fact that over 300,000 women in the workplace are involved in a wide range of occupations and industries. Portrayal of the woman at home is often that of an unintelligent, dimwitted human being, without any interests or involvement outside the home (e.g. soap powder and margarine advertisements). When advertising does refer to women in jobs outside the home, traditional ones are usually shown (e.g. receptionist, typist, shop assistant). This type of treatment is known as sex-stereotyping.

Secondly, criticism is made of the use of women's bodies to sell products. Women are treated as sex objects in advertisements which degrade and undermine their equal status. The most blatant examples of this type of advertising are for motor cars, diets and tights. Apart from being offensive and degrading to women this type of advertising can have bad effects on the overall attitudes of society towards violence against women.

The ICTU has recommended that advertisements:

(a) fairly reflect women's role in society,
(b) restrain the degrading use of women's bodies to sell products,
(c) avoid the use of sexual innuendo.

Participation of Women in the Media

Criticism has been made by the ICTU of the limited participation of women in certain areas of the media. The use of women as experts or commentators on current affairs is rare and, when they are used it tends to be on subjects related to social issues rather than economic or political ones. Women rarely feature in a debate on the economy or unemployment. Very often issues of concern to women are side-tracked into a corner — either on the women's page of newspapers or to special radio or television women's programmes. While the feature pages and special programmes are useful in highlighting women's issues, they should not be used as a substitute for dealing with these issues in the general context of public interest. Matters which affect women affect a large proportion (50 percent) of the population and therefore should not be treated merely as a minority interest.

Questions

1. Complete these sentences:
    (a) The term media refers to . . . . .
    (b) The public generally only sees or hears about major industrial disputes on . . . . .
    (c) Routine work of unions is seldom . . . . .
    (d) Generally the media only begin to cover a dispute when . . . . .
    (e) Good news is rarely as . . . . . as bad news.

2. State whether each statement is true or false. If false correct the statement.
   (a) Media coverage of union activities concentrates mainly on industrial disputes.
   (b) Everyone reads detailed newspaper accounts of industrial disputes.
   (c) Many unions publish their own newsletters.
   (d) The ICTU is satisfied with the treatment of women in advertising.
   (e) Sex stereotyping presents a fixed and unchanging view of women in society.

3. Examine as many morning, evening and Sunday newspapers as you can get over the next week. Make a collection of articles covering union affairs and industrial disputes, then consider them as follows:
   (a) What impression do the headlines give?
   (b) How detailed an account is given of the causes of industrial disputes?
   (c) Is there a bias or slant in the coverage?
   (d) Compare how the same dispute is reported in different papers.
   (e) What impression do you get of unions from reading these reports?

4. Write to one or more of the large trade unions and ask them for a copy of their union newsletter. Then compare their reports of union activities to those in the daily newspapers.

5. Select one of the following statements and give your opinion on it. You may agree or disagree with the statement but give reasons.
   (a) 'Television coverage of union disputes is very poor. Unions are usually shown in a bad light. The cameras just pick out sensational events and only report what is startling and strange.'
   (b) 'Bad news helps to sell papers. People don't want to read about the good things that unions do, that's why reporters don't write about them.'
   (c) 'Everyone likes looking at attractive women. Advertisements without them would be boring. Women choose to appear in advertisements and get well paid for them. I'm against censorship — keep advertisements the way they are.'

6. Carry out a survey on the treatment of women in advertisements. Cut out advertisements from newspapers and magazines. Consider how women are shown:

   (a) as housewives   (d) as sex objects to sell products
   (b) working in traditional jobs (e) as simple minded individuals
   (c) working in non-traditional jobs

   What impressions are conveyed in each case? Write a report on your findings.

7. When you have studied one of the case studies in this book:
   (a) write a newspaper article on it
   (b) devise a two minute report.
   Include scenes you would show and comment to accompany them. Then compare and contrast the coverage in each case.

Role-play/Discussion

A Conference has been organised on the topic of 'Women and Advertising'. Various speakers have been invited to address an interested audience. The panel of speakers includes a spokesperson from each of the following:

(a) an advertising agency   (d) The Consumers' Association
(b) a women's group   (e) A soap powder firm
(c) the ICTU Women's Committee (f) RTE management

After contributions from each of these speakers there will be an opportunity for contributions and questions from the floor. Discuss/role-play this situation.

19 · Young People and the Law

THE PROTECTION OF YOUNG PERSONS (EMPLOYMENT) ACT 1977

This is the main law covering the employment of young people. The Act applies generally to young workers under eighteen years of age. Under this Act, a 'young person' means someone aged fifteen but under eighteen years of age, and a 'child' means a person under school-leaving age, at present fifteen years.

Minimum Age of Employment

It is illegal to employ any child under fourteen years of age. Employment between fourteen and fifteen years of age is generally not allowed. As an exception to this a child, over fourteen and under fifteen years, may be allowed to do light non-industrial work during school holidays. This is only allowed when the work is not harmful to health or normal development and does not interfere with his/her schooling. The working hours of children during school holidays should not be more than seven hours in any day, or 35 hours in any week. During school summer holidays a child must not do any work for one full period of fourteen days. Children over fourteen may not be employed during school term, apart from second-level students taking part in work experience or other courses arranged or agreed by the Minister for Education.

Hours of Work

The limits on hours of work are as follows:

1. Young Persons aged between fifteen and sixteen years

	Normal Working Hours	Maximum Hours of Work
In any day	8	8
In any week	37½	40

2. Young Persons aged between sixteen and eighteen years

	Normal Working Hours	Maximum Hours of Work
In any day	8	9
In any week	40	45
In any four weeks	—	172
In any year	—	2,000

Time spent with the employer's permission in vocational training during normal hours counts as working time within the limits of maximum hours. Furthermore, a worker's wages cannot be reduced where a reduction in hours is necessary under the terms as set out in this Act.

Double Employment

An employer must not allow an employee to work for him on any day on which s/he has worked for another employer. An exception to this is where the total number of hours worked is not more than the daily maximum hourly limits for one employer.

Hours of work for young people are regulated by legislation.

Night Work

The employment of children under school-leaving age (at present fifteen years) is not allowed between the hours of 8.00 p.m. and 8.00 a.m. In addition, there must be an interval of fourteen hours from the time a child finishes work to the time s/he starts again.

Young persons aged fifteen but under eighteen years are not allowed to do any work between the hours of 10.00 p.m. and 8.00 a.m. There must also be an interval of twelve hours between work finishing and starting times. This does not apply to industrial workers, who must not be employed between 8.00 p.m. and 8.00 a.m.

Rest Periods

Employees must be given at least 24 hours continuous rest in every seven days. This applies to those who work more than five days a week and who work on a Sunday for more than three hours.

The 1972 regulations state that the employer must provide or arrange for the supervision of, and the training or instruction in, any process which involves lifting or carrying. This is to safeguard health and to prevent accidents.

Questions

1. Complete these sentences:
   (a) The main law covering the employment of young people is .....
   (b) It is an offence for an employer to employ anyone under eighteen years of age without first .....
   (c) It is illegal to employ any child under .....
   (d) During school summer holidays a child (fourteen to fifteen years) must not do any work for .....
   (e) According to the law, the heaviest weight a seventeen-year-old boy should be asked to lift at work is .....

2. Select the correct answer in each case.
   (a) Under the law the maximum hours of work, per week, for a fifteen-and-a-half-year-old are:
       (i) 35   (ii) 37½   (iii) 40   (iv) none of these.
   (b) Under the law the maximum hours of work for a seventeen-year-old are:
       (i) 40   (ii) 46   (iii) 50   (iv) none of these.
   (c) For young people, overtime payment rate must be not less than the normal rate increased by:
       (i) 20 percent   (ii) 25 percent   (iii) 50 percent   (iv) none of these.
   (d) Shift work in a brewery must not be longer than:
       (i) eight hours   (ii) nine hours   (iii) ten hours   (iv) none of these.
   (e) The maximum weight a seventeen-year-old girl is legally allowed to lift at work is:
       (i) 24.2 lbs   (ii) 27.6 lbs   (iii) 35.1 lbs   (iv) none of these.

3. State whether each statement is true or false. If false correct the statement.
   (a) Under the Protection of Young Persons (Employment) Act, 1977, a 'young person' means someone aged fifteen to eighteen years of age.
   (b) The daily working time of a fourteen-and-a-half-year-old boy during school summer holidays should not be more than 8 hours.
   (c) The normal working hours of a seventeen-year-old girl should not be more than forty hours per week.
   (d) Under no circumstances can a young person work for two different employers on the same day.
   (e) In an electricity generating station a worker is allowed to work two shifts together.

124

4. Explain these terms:
   — Non-industrial work   — Shift-work
   — Overtime pay   — Continuous process industry
   — Double employment

5. Select one of these opinions and comment on it:
   (a) 'The law is very complicated and generally on the side of the employers. Unions shouldn't waste time dealing with it, but should get on with the job of fighting for better pay and conditions.'
   (b) 'The school-leaving age of fifteen is too low. Fifteen-year-olds are immature and not well enough prepared for life and the world of work. The school-leaving age should be raised to sixteen and eventually to eighteen.'
   (c) 'Trade unions need to spend more time looking for changes in the law as applied to the employment of young people. At present the law gives them only minimal protection.'

6. (a) Laws are constantly kept under review and changed from time to time. Select a regulation, from this chapter, which you think should be changed and say why.
   (b) In your opinion, is there a need to introduce any new law for young persons in any of the following areas: the minimum age of employment, hours of work, night work or overtime? Give reasons for your answer.

Role-play/Further discussion

A large brewery recruited new employees. Two of them played on the same soccer team as a shop steward in the brewery. Before starting there, the new workers were keen to find out what the shift-work regulations were. One evening after a training session they had a chat with the shop steward about this. He told them what the regulations were and that, although they were in line with the law, his union wanted changes, particularly to provide for more rest periods during shifts. Role-play/discuss and develop the situation.

20 · Pay, Holidays and Dismissal

PAYMENT OF WAGES

Under the laws covering the payment of wages the following regulations apply:

1. All employees are entitled to receive a wage slip at the same time as they receive their wages. Wage slips must show clearly the amounts of, and the reasons for, all deductions from the gross wages.

2. Deductions from wages must be strictly according to contracts of employment or special regulations for manual workers.

3. Manual workers must be paid in cash, unless they agree to non-cash (e.g. cheque) methods of payment.

HOLIDAY REGULATIONS

The right to holidays is covered by the Holidays (Employees) Act (1973). This Act gives workers the right to a minimum period of both paid annual holidays and public holidays. The main regulations are as follows:

1. Generally workers are legally entitled to at least three weeks annual holidays and eight days public holidays.

2. The right to annual holidays depends on actual hours worked including overtime.

3. To get full annual holidays you must work for the same employer for 1,400 hours (i.e. 40 hours a week for 35 weeks). If you are under eighteen years the requirement is 1,300 hours. For most people, the Act entitles them to $1\frac{1}{4}$ days holidays for each month worked (120 hours).

4. Holiday pay has to be paid at the same rate as a person's average earnings, less overtime pay.

5. Under this Act the employer can decide when holidays are to be taken.

6. For public holidays there is no qualifying period required for workers, other than part-time or day-to-day workers. For part-time and day-to-day workers, the Act requires that 120 hours must be worked in the five weeks ending the day before the holiday.

UNFAIR DISMISSAL

Under the Unfair Dismissals Act (1977), protection is given to workers who have been unfairly dismissed by their employer. All dismissals are regarded as being unfair and the employer is required to prove that sufficient reasons existed in the circumstances for dismissal to take place. The following are the main provisions of the Act:

1. Generally if you have worked for your employer for one full year you are protected against unfair dismissal, provided you have worked at least twenty hours per week. The following groups are not covered by the Act: government employees, gardai, defence forces, Local Authority officers, Health Board and Vocational Education Committee employees.

2. You are protected by the Act if you are dismissed for trade union activity or because of pregnancy, even though you haven't given one year's service to your employer.

3. If your employer has failed to observe an adequate disciplinary or dismissals procedure your dismissal is regarded as unfair.

4. Unfair dismissal cases are dealt with by a Rights Commissioner and/or the Employment Appeals Tribunal.

5. Claims under the Unfair Dismissals Act must be brought within six months.

6. The remedies available to workers found to be unfairly dismissed are reinstatement (getting the same job back), re-engagement (getting another job with the same employer) or compensation.

7. The maximum amount of compensation which can be awarded under this Act is two years' gross pay. Compensation can be reduced where a worker is found to have been at fault.

Minimum Notice in Dismissal Cases

Whether or not a dismissal is unfair, most workers are entitled to a proper period of notice. The regulations for proper notice are given in the Minimum Notice and Terms of Employment Act (1973). This Act entitles most workers who have had continuous employment of at least thirteen weeks with the same employer and worked at least eighteeen hours per week, to a minimum of notice.

The main terms of the Act are as follows:

1. The period of notice required is based on the length of service, as follows:

Length of Service	Period of Notice
13 weeks-2 years	1 week
2 years-5 years	2 weeks
5 years-10 years	4 weeks
10 years-15 years	6 weeks
over 15 years	8 weeks

2. Notice may be spoken or written, but must be given directly to the employee.

3. An employer must give an employee wages to cover the period of notice.

4. Claims for dismissal without proper notice can be brought to the Employment Appeals Tribunal. There is a time limit of six years for bringing claims.

5. Workers who are dismissed without the proper notice may be awarded compensation under this Act. Compensation will only be awarded for such period of notice as the worker was *available for work*.

REDUNDANCY ARRANGEMENTS

The Redundancy Acts ensure that redundant workers receive some financial compensation. The Redundancy Acts make the following provisions:

1. Most workers who have worked continuously for the same employer for at least *two years* and are normally expected to work *at least eighteen hours* for that employer are covered by the Redundancy Acts.

2. Redundancy can occur when an employer's need for workers to do a particular kind of work in a particular place either diminishes or ceases.

3. Entitlement to redundancy payment depends on a worker actually being dismissed.

4. There is no entitlement to a redundancy payment where suitable alternative work is offered and there is no good reason to refuse it.

5. The size of a redundancy payment under the Acts depends on age, length of service and gross normal weekly pay. The minimum entitlement of a worker is:
   gross normal weekly (subject to a maximum clause)
   plus
   half of the gross weekly pay for every year of continuous employment between sixteen and 41 years of age,
   plus
   a gross normal week's pay for every year of continuous service after 41 years of age.

6. Lump sums are paid by the employer, who can then claim a rebate from the Redundancy Fund. If the employer cannot pay, the lump sum is paid out of the Redundancy Fund.

7. Disputes about redundancy entitlement are dealt with by the Employment Appeals Tribunal. Disputes should be referred to the Tribunal not later than a year after the date of dismissal. This period may be extended by the Tribunal, where the employer has breached the legal rulings of the Act.

Questions

1. Complete these sentences:
   (a) Manual workers must be paid in cash unless . . . . .
   (b) Generally workers are legally entitled to at least three weeks annual holidays and . . . . .
   (c) Holiday pay has to be paid at the same rate as . . . . .
   (d) An unfair dismissal case can be taken to . . . . .

(e) If you have worked for the same employer for three years the minimum dismissal notice is . . . . .

(f) Disputes about redundancy entitlements are dealt with by . . . . .

2. Say whether each of these statements is true or false. If false, correct the statement.

    (a) All employees are entitled to receive a wage slip at the same time as they get their wages.

    (b) If you are over eighteen, to get full annual holidays you must have worked for the same employer for at least 1,400 hours.

    (c) A soldier in the Irish army is not covered by the Unfair Dismissals Act (1977).

    (d) If you have worked full-time for an employer for one year you are entitled to a day's dismissal notice.

    (e) You must have worked at least eighteen hours per week for two years to be fully covered by the Redundancy Acts.

3. In each case select the correct answer.

    (a) Under the Holidays Act most people are entitled to $1\frac{1}{4}$ days annual holidays for working each:
    (i) week   (ii) fortnight   (iii) month   (iv) none of these.

    (b) After a dismissal a claim under the Unfair Dismissal Act must be brought within:
    (i) six weeks   (ii) six months   (iii) six years   (iv) none of these.

    (c) The maximum amount of compensation which can be awarded under the Unfair Dismissals Act (1977) is your gross pay for:
    (i) one month   (ii) one year   (iii) three years   (iv) none of these.

    (d) If you have worked full-time for an employer for three years you are entitled to a minimum dismissal notice of:
    (i) two weeks   (ii) three weeks   (iii) four weeks   (iv) none of these.

    (c) Disputes about redundancy entitlement are dealt with by:
    (i) The Labour Court   (ii) A Rights Commissioner   (iii) The Employment Appeals Tribunal   (iv) none of these.

4. Under the Holidays (Employees) Act (1973), most workers are entitled to three weeks annual holidays and eight days public holidays. Using a calendar, find out the dates of the public holidays.

5. Explain these terms:
— Non-cash payment   — Reinstatement
— Day-to-day work   — Unfair dismissal
— Continuous service   — Redundancy payment

6. (a) A worker can take an unfair dismissal case to a Rights Commissioner and/or the Employment Appeals Tribunal. If a worker is found to

have been unfairly dismissed, what remedies are available to him/her?

(b) In your opinion, what are the advantages and disadvantages of the Minimum Notice and Terms of Employment Act (1973)?

7. Select one of these opinions and comment on it.

(a) 'Under the Holidays Act an employer can decide when holidays are to be taken. I think that the workers and their unions should be consulted about the timing of and arrangements for all holidays.'

(b) 'The Unfair Dismissals Act (1977) makes it very difficult for someone to be sacked.'

(c) 'The Redundancy Acts don't provide enough compensation for workers who are laid off.'

Role-play/Further discussion

John was a shop steward in a plastics factory. He had been with the firm just over five years. He was popular with the other workers and spent a lot of his spare time dealing with their questions and problems. Sometimes he had to deal with union matters during his working hours. His boss didn't like this and regularly checked his work.

One day along with his pay-packet John was handed a letter giving him two weeks' dismissal notice. When he asked about the reasons for this he was told that his work was unsatisfactory and below the standard required by the firm. John was very angry and decided not to take this treatment lying down. Role-play/discuss this situation.

21 · Equality

EQUAL PAY FOR EQUAL WORK

The Anti-Discrimination (Pay) Act 1974 provides for equal pay between men and women, if they are doing *'like work'*. The Act applies to all workers, including temporary and part-time workers. To bring a successful equal pay claim under the Act, the following requirements are laid down:

1. The claim must be based on a comparison between men and women working for the *same employer* or an *associated employer*. Employers are associated where one is controlled by another, or if both are controlled by a third.

2. A comparison must be made between men and women working in the *'same place'*. The same place includes a city, town or locality — not just the same factory or office.

3. To bring an equal pay claim under the Act, men and women must be doing *'like work'*. This means:

   (a) the *same work* done under the same or similar conditions;
   (b) *similar work* where the differences between the work carried out or the conditions under which it is done by each are of small importance;
   (c) *work of equal value*, in terms of the demands it makes in such matters as skill, physical or mental effort, responsibility or working conditions. This could cover situations where the work and working conditions of the men and women are totally different e.g. an office worker and a factory worker.

4. The Act allows employers to pay different rates to workers who are doing *'like work'*, provided this is *'on grounds other than sex'*. For example, years of service could lead to different rates of pay for workers doing the same work.

5. Equal pay claims should first be made to the employer. Where negotiations fail, the claim may then be brought to an Equality Officer.

6. Equality Officers will investigate the claim. In carrying out the investigation, they may visit the workplace, examine records and documents, seek information and inspect work.

7. Following the investigation the Equality Officer will issue a Recommendation.

8. The Officer's decision may be appealed to the Labour Court within 42 days of the Recommendation being issued. Either side may appeal.

9. If the employer refuses to implement the Recommendation, an appeal may be made to the Labour Court within 42 days.

10. Having considered the matter, the Labour Court will issue its findings on the Appeal.

11. The Department of Labour can prosecute employers in the District Court for not carrying out the ruling of the Labour Court.

12. A successful claim under the Act may be backdated to apply three years before it is made to the Equality Officer.

WHAT THE LAW SAYS ABOUT DISCRIMINATION

The Employment Equality Act (1977) makes it illegal for an employer to discriminate on grounds of sex or of marital status in employment. The Act is aimed at abolishing such discrimination. Employers are forbidden to discriminate in respect of any of the following:

1. *Recruitment* This covers everything from job advertising to interviews and rules for selection.

2. *Conditions of employment* This covers all aspects of the job — the terms on which the job is offered, the physical working conditions, basic hours, overtime, shift-work, lay-offs, transfers, dismissals and discipline.

3. *Training* All aspects of training and work experience are covered. Under the Act positive discrimination is allowed. Employers or training organisations are allowed to encourage members of either sex to go into non-traditional areas of work, e.g. men into nursing, women into engineering.

4. *Promotion* Employers cannot discriminate in this area.

5. *Classifying jobs* It is unlawful to classify jobs according to sex, unless the sex of job holders is an occupational qualification e.g. in modelling or in acting.

6. *Rules, Instructions and Practices* Under the Act, employers are forbidden to make rules, give instructions or operate practices which either directly or indirectly involve inferior treatment of individuals or groups of people of a particular sex or marital status.

7. *Claims* of discrimination should be taken up first with the employer. If no agreement is reached with the employer, then a written complaint should be made to the Labour Court. This must be done within six months of the first occasion on which the discrimination took place.

8. *The Labour Court* may refer the case to an Equality Officer straight away or to an Industrial Relations Officer who will try to settle the matter. If the latter fails, the case then goes to an Equality Officer.

9. *The Equality Officer* carries out an investigation and issues a Recommendation. Appeals against the Recommendation must be made within 42 days and must state the grounds of appeal.

WHAT THE EMPLOYMENT EQUALITY AGENCY DOES

The Employment Equality Agency was set up under the Employment Equality Act (1977). The Agency acts as a watchdog in the area of discrimination and its job is to:

1. work towards the elimination of discrimination in employment;

2. promote equality of opportunity between men and women;

3. review the operation of the Anti-Discrimination (Pay) Act and the Employment Equality Act.

above: The creche at RTE opened in 1987 after years of campaigning by the trade unions

below: Trade unions conduct important campaigns for the rights of all workers. The ICTU is campaigning for the implementation of its Charter for Disabled Workers.

The Agency itself can take legal action against people and organisations who practice discrimination. It can also help individuals who have suffered discrimination.

WHAT ABOUT MATERNITY PROTECTION?

The Maternity Protection of Employees Act (1981) provides for maternity leave. Once a woman is employed for twenty-six weeks (or under a fixed-term contract for less) and is insured for social welfare, she is covered by the Act. The following are the main terms of the Act:

1. *Length of Leave* The Act provides for fourteen weeks paid maternity leave and a further option of four weeks unpaid leave. This leave doesn't affect other types of leave, e.g. holidays or sick leave. It can be taken as the woman wishes provided that at least four weeks are taken before the expected date of birth and at least four weeks are taken after the birth. These are the normal requirements but some flexibility is allowed.

2. *Notification to Employer* The woman wishing to take maternity leave must notify her employer in writing, at least four weeks before the leave is due to start. She must supply a medical certificate stating the expected date of birth. If she wishes to extend her maternity leave (maximum four weeks, unpaid) she must notify her employer in writing as soon as possible.

3. *Right to Return to Work* The Act gives a woman who has taken maternity leave the right to return to work if she wishes to do so. She is entitled to return to the same job, under the same conditions. The employer can offer 'suitable alternative employment under a new contract', if returning to the original job is not 'reasonably practicable'. Any such alternative employment must be (a) suitable and appropriate for the person concerned and (b) the conditions must not be 'substantially less favourable' than the original ones.

4. *Preservation of Rights* Employers must preserve all of a woman's rights while she is on paid maternity leave e.g. pension rights and special allowances.

5. *Maternity Pay* There is a maternity allowance scheme under the social welfare system to cover the area of maternity pay. A woman should receive a weekly amount which corresponds to her average net earnings. A minimum level of benefit exists.

SPECIAL PROTECTIVE LEGISLATION FOR WOMEN

While there are laws to ensure equal pay for equal work and to make sex discrimination in employment illegal, special protective laws for women cover conditions of work and types of employment. The following are the laws which apply at present:

1. *Shops (Conditions of Employment) Act, 1938*
   Under this Act, employers must provide at least one seat behind the counter for every three female sales staff.

2. *The Factories Act, 1955*
   This Act lays down different weight-lifting limits for men and women as follows:

Age	Maximum Male	Weight Female
Under 16	17.6 lbs	17.6 lbs
Under 18	35.2 lbs	24.2 lbs
Over 18	121.0 lbs	35.2 lbs

   The Act also forbids women from cleaning moving machinery and completely excludes them from certain types of work which involve a health hazard, such as zinc processing, lead and lead compound manufacture. In addition, females under eighteen cannot be employed in certain glass manufacture and salt extraction work.

3. *The Mines and Quarries Act, 1965*
   This Act forbids women general workers from working below ground at a mine. Women doing non-manual work may go underground. In the case of women working above ground they must have at least a twelve-hour break between each working period, seven hours of which must be between 10.00 p.m. and 7.00 a.m. This legislation is currently under review and this prohibition may be removed.

Questions

1. Complete these sentences:
   (a) The Act which provides for equal pay for equal work is called . . . . .
   (b) Equal pay claims should first be made to . . . . .
   (c) An Equality Officer investigates . . . . .
   (d) The Employment Equality Agency promotes employment equality for . . . . .
   (e) Under the law the maximum weight a woman worker over eighteen is allowed to lift is . . . . .

2. Say whether each of these statements is true or false. If false correct the statement.
   (a) The Anti-Discrimination (Pay) Act, 1974, does not apply to temporary or part-time workers.

(b) The rules of the Employment Equality Act cover the wording of job advertisements.

(c) Under no legal circumstances can men and women doing 'like work' receive different rates of pay.

(d) You can be barred from taking part in a training course because of your sex.

(e) The Employment Equality Agency has no power, it can only make complaints.

3. In each case select the correct answer:
   (a) The Employment Equality Act (1977) makes it illegal to discriminate on grounds of:
       (i) race   (ii) religion   (iii) sex   (iv) none of these.
   (b) After an Equality Officer's Recommendation is issued, an appeal against it may be made to the Labour Court within:
       (i) 42 days   (ii) one year   (iii) two years   (iv) none of these.
   (c) The watchdog agency which specifically works towards the elimination of sex discrimination in employment is the:
       (i) Employer-Labour Conference   (ii) Labour Court   (iii) Employment Equality Agency   (iv) none of these.
   (d) To qualify for full maternity leave a pregnant woman must work at least eighteen hours a week and be employed for at least:
       (i) three months   (ii) four weeks   (iii) six months   (iv) none of these.

4. Explain these terms, giving examples where possible:
   — Sex discrimination   — Reverse discrimination
   — Equality of opportunity   — 'Work of equal value'
   — Paid leave

5. (a) List the jobs which women under law are forbidden from doing.
   (b) In your opinion should women be forbidden from doing certain types of work? Give reasons for your answer.

6. Select one of these opinions and comment on it:
   (a) 'All this talk about equality between the sexes is alright, but there are certain jobs which men can do better than women and vice versa.'
   (b) 'There's no point in making sex discrimination illegal, if girls haven't got the proper qualifications for all jobs. Girls must have the same educational choices as boys, if they are to have the same employment opportunities later on.'
   (c) 'Paid maternity leave, good childcare facilities and the elimination of all forms of discrimination should make it possible for women to continue in their jobs when they have children.'

(d) 'If women can get maternity leave, is there not a case for men getting paternity leave?'

7. Karen worked on the reception desk in a large supermarket. She was very experienced at her job, having worked before in different sections. She was ambitious and willing to take on more responsibility. During the past year she had done two management courses. When a vacancy arose for an assistant managerial position she applied. After an interview she felt confident about her prospects of getting the job. However, to her amazement, a man with much less experience was appointed. She wasn't sure, but she suspected that because she was a woman she might have been passed over.

Describe what someone in Karen's position could do, outlining the course of action where sex discrimination is suspected.

8. What other minority groups need protection against discrimination in the workplace?

Role-play/Further discussion

A trade union conference is being organised for union members on the topic 'Employment Equality'. A panel of speakers, including representatives from the Department of Labour, Department of Education, Federated Union of Employers, Employment Equality Agency and the ICTU, has been invited. There will be speeches and opportunities for contributions and questions from the floor. Role-play/discuss this situation.

22 · Health and Safety

There are many ways in which workers can be injured or their health damaged in factories or other workplaces. The following are some common causes of workplace injuries and of dangers to health:

— Dangerous chemicals, e.g. acids, pesticides, glues
— Fire hazards, e.g. highly inflammable material
— Noise, e.g. heavy machinery
— Electrical wiring and equipment
— Gases, e.g. exhaust fumes
— Dust, e.g. asbestos dust
— Dangerous machinery or equipment
— Bad workplace design and layout (ergonomics).

Trade unions have long campaigned for proper safety procedures, safety inspection and protective legislation covering the health and safety of all workers. There are three main pieces of legislation covering this area:

The Factories Act, 1955	covers health and safety standards mainly in factories.
The Office Premises Act, 1958	covers health and safety standards in workplaces with a minimum of six clerical workers.
The Safety in Industry Act, 1980	updates the Factories Act, 1955 and makes provision for workers' involvement in safety and health at their workplaces.

The ICTU sees the need for a major extension of safety and health legislation to cover all workers. At present only about 20 percent of the workforce is covered, while thousands of workers employed in agriculture, schools, hospitals, fisheries and forestry are not.

Industrial Accidents

Provisional figures made available by the Industrial Inspectorate of the Department of Labour show that in the twelve months to September 1987 there were 3,166 industrial accidents reported to the Department. The quarterly figures were as follows:

Fourth Quarter 1986	848
First Quarter 1987	756 (3 fatal)
Second Quarter 1987	782 (2 fatal)
Third Quarter 1987	780 (4 fatal)

Of the nine fatal accidents, four occurred in the construction industry and two in the food, drink and tobacco industry.

The biggest number of accidents occurred in the food, drink and tobacco industry (690), followed by the construction industry (295).

In the year to September 1987 there were, on average, thirteen *reported* accidents on every working day.

It is to be noted that only accidents involving absences of more than three days are reported to the Industrial Inspectorate and that the existing legislation on industrial safety applies to only one-fourth of the workforce.

Exposed to Risks

Under our present inadequate and outdated occupational health and safety system, thousands of Irish workers are exposed daily to serious health and

295 accidents were reported in the construction industry in 1987.

safety risks. Workers are handling dangerous substances and dealing with new technologies which involve unknown risks to their health and safety. Most accidents and health problems do not arise from workers' carelessness. Carelessness does not explain ill-health and accidents caused by dust, noise, toxic fumes and unsafe systems of work. Occupational health and safety aims to prevent accidents and damage to health and to promote welfare in the workplace. According to the Barrington Commission, 'occupationl health is not simply a matter of eliminating lethal and disabling industrial diseases . . . it is concerned not merely with the effect of work on health but also with the need to promote the health and working capacity of the worker and to adapt work methods, procedures and working conditions to a person's state of health . . . Occupational health views people in the context of their work and their working environment, in other words in full knowledge of the products and processes with which they have been working.'

Management Responsibility

It is the responsibility of management to ensure a safe and healthy workplace. Unfortunately, health and safety is seen as an 'extra' by most employers and inevitably suffers with cut-backs. Congress believes that occupational health and safety can be cost effective — both in terms of workers' health and employers' costs — by eliminating the hazards which create the health and safety problems.

Need for Reform

The workforce of today has a more informed and concerned approach towards its health and safety. This growing awareness amongst workers of the importance of a safe and healthy work environment demands a response from employers, Government and trade unions. Central to the recommendations and overall thrust of the Barrington Report was the proposal for a framework Act which would set down fundamental principles covering all workplaces and all workers. In the Programme for National Recovery, Congress received a commitment from Government that a Framework Bill to give effect to the main recommendations of the Barrington Commission would be brought before the Oireachtas in 1988. This Bill will put in place a radically new health and safety system. Congress and its affiliated unions will be undertaking an education and training programme to ensure that workers will benefit fully from such a new system.

Questions

1. Complete the following sentences:
   (a) The Factories Act, 1955 covers health and safety standards mainly in
       . . . . .
   (b) The Office Premises Act was passed in . . . . .
   (c) The Safety in Industry Act, 1980 makes provision for . . . . .

2. List four of the common causes of workplace injuries and dangers to health.

3. How many industrial accidents were reported to the Department of Labour in the twelve months to September 1987?

4. How many fatal accidents occurred in the construction industry in the year to September 1987?

5. Say whether each statement is true or false. If false, correct the statement.
   (a) According to the Barrington Commission, 'occupational health is simply a matter of eliminating lethal and disabling industrial diseases.'
   (b) The ICTU says that most accidents and health problems at work arise from workers' carelessness.
   (c) In the year to September 1987 there were, on average, thirteen reported accidents on every working day.
   (d) Only accidents involving absence of more than one day are reported to the Industrial Inspectorate.

6. The following are some examples of the type of problems which a Safety Committee or a Safety Representative would deal with:
   — very loud noise from machines which could damage hearing;
   — irritation and damage to skin from dangerous chemicals;
   — threat of fire outbreak from presence of highly inflammable fuel.
   In each case suggest recommendations for eliminating the threat or danger (e.g. soundproofing to reduce loud noise).

7. A Safety Committee has recommended to an employer that warning notices should be placed around the factory premises pointing out the danger to workers of not wearing ear muffs when using noisy machines. Design a poster, suitable for display, to persuade workers to use the ear muffs provided.

Role-play/Further discussion

Colorine is a paint manufacturer employing 92 people. Concern has been expressed about the fire safety standards in the factory, which have resulted in loss of life and serious injuries. A meeting of the Safety Committee is held to discuss the matter. Among the items discussed are the provision and adequacy of fire alarms, escapes, extinguishers, hoses, sprinkler heads, first aid kits, fire blankets, fire drills, warning notices and organisation of fire evacuations. Contributions to the discussion are made by both worker and employer representatives. Role-play/discuss this situation, giving recommendations as to what needs to be done.

Case Study 1

THE WAGE CLAIM

Encon Ltd. is a multi-national company with a plant in Ireland employing 600 workers. The company is involved in the production of parts for the computer industry. There are three unions representing workers in the Irish plant: a general union, a craft union and a white-collar union.

In September 1987, the unions put in a wage and salary claim for an increase of 13 percent in the basic rates of all workers. Management had five meetings with the unions and made an offer of 6 percent. This offer was rejected by the unions by a ballot vote. 427 voted against the offer and 120 voted in favour. The unions requested the Labour Court to investigate the dispute. Three conciliation conferences were held but the two sides failed to reach a settlement.

On the recommendation of an Industrial Relations Officer, the unions and management agreed to request the Labour Court to investigate the dispute. In its submission to the court, the main argument put forward by the unions was the increase in the cost of living of 13 percent, and that workers were entitled to compensation to protect their standard of living. Management put forward the argument that due to the international recession they could not afford to pay the increase being sought by the unions.

When asked by the chairman of the court for information on the trading position of the company, management stated that this information could only be supplied by the company's headquarters in Dallas, Texas.

In its recommendation, the court stated that due to the failure of the company to supply the court with the up-to-date trading position, the court could only recommend that the union and management should start direct negotiations again and that the company should provide the unions with the relevant financial information. Both unions and management accepted the court recommendation.

The unions and the company held five meetings in December to discuss the wage claim. At these meetings, the company failed to produce the information on their trading position, claiming that they were having difficulty receiving this from their headquarters.

At the last meeting the management made a final offer of 7 percent and felt that this was all they could do to meet the union's claim. A meeting of the union's members was arranged to consider the final offer of management. Prior to the meeting with all of the members, the union official met with the shop steward and the research officer from the General Union and provided the meeting with the following information.

1. That enquiries made in other countries concerning the operations of the company had yielded no evidence that the company is suffering from the effects of the recession.

2. That the components being produced by the company are being sold in an expanding market.

3. That other companies in the same industrial sector have made offers of between 12 percent and 14 percent to their workers.

Note to Students

Examine the case as outlined. Discuss in groups and identify any questions concerning the case which you are not clear about or about the system of Industrial Relations. Please note the following options which were considered by the union officials and the shop steward to resolve the wage claim:

1. Reject the offer and request a further meeting with the management.

2. Request the union to take the issue back to the Labour Court.

3. Request the union to sanction industrial action.

4. Request the union also to make application for an all-out picket from the Irish Congress of Trade Unions.

5. The workers consider taking immediate unofficial action against the company.

6. Accept the offer of 7 percent.

Which of these solutions would you recommend?

Case Study 2

DISCRIMINATION

Maeve is seventeen years of age. It is over six months since she left her local convent school. She has been working for most of this time for a large supermarket. There are over eighty assistants employed by the store, twenty of whom are girls under eighteen years of age. A new neighbour of Maeve's, Aidan, works in the office of the same supermarket and is also seventeen years old.

Shop assistants in the supermarket work from 9.00 a.m. to 6.00 p.m. from Mondays to Fridays. They have to work a full day on one Saturday a month. They also have to work until 9.00 p.m. on every second Thursday and every second Friday. Clerical workers work from 9.00 a.m. to 5.15 p.m., Monday to Friday.

Aidan is training to become a manager and goes one day a week to a technical college in the city for a course in management. The college also offers a course in marketing on the same day. As Maeve would like to become involved in sales promotion she has sought permission to attend the marketing course.

Her supervisor, Miss Clancy, resents the fact that Maeve is seeking this 'privilege'. Shop assistants are not given release from work for training. Miss Clancy tells Maeve that she will not be given permission and criticises her for even asking. She claims that Maeve knew that the supermarket did not allow such release to shop assistants. Maeve is angry with the manner in which Miss Clancy has treated her. She is also angry with Aidan, who works shorter hours, and is given study leave while she is not. She complains to Miss Clancy, saying that the shop assistants, who are all female, are being discriminated against. An argument follows and afterwards Maeve is sent for by the personnel manager. Mr O'Reilly, the personnel manager, takes Miss Clancy's side. He threatens to dismiss Maeve unless she apologises to Miss Clancy and forgets about the training course.

Maeve goes immediately to see Deirdre, her shop steward. Deirdre has been trying for a long time to get release for training for any girls working as shop assistants who wish to avail of it. She asks to see Mr O'Reilly to discuss Maeve's case.

ROLE PLAY — CHARACTERS

The Supervisor

Miss Clancy is 35 years old and has worked for the store all her working life. She never had the chance to train further but still managed to become supervisor. She thinks young girls are well paid for the work they do and that conditions at work are much better than they used to be. She is always under pressure because the trade in the store has increased and they are always short of shop assistants. She is also a member of the union.

The Personnel Manager

Mr O'Reilly is a young man from university with little experience of handling workers' problems. The manager of the store is always telling him that he must keep the store properly supplied with shop assistants. He knows that the supervisor is a little unhappy and he is afraid that if he doesn't back her she will leave. On the other hand, he thinks that those girls who want to train to better themselves ought to be encouraged. Perhaps a part-time assistant to cover Maeve's absence might be the answer.

The Shop Steward

Deirdre is a shop assistant. She is a young married woman and is 27 years old. She understands the supervisor's problems but thinks the management of the store should employ more staff. Deirdre used to work in the local council office where day-release was available for all young employees, not only the clerical staff. She has often told the Personnel Officer that day-release should be given to the young girls serving in the store. The store would benefit from this in the long run. She is surprised that Ms Foy, the Manager, is not more concerned with improving the lot of the female staff.

The Manager

Ms Foy thinks that getting extra staff would increase her costs and anyway, reliable staff are difficult to find. If one girl goes off to be trained, others may get the same idea, and no one will be satisfied with being an ordinary shop assistant. A number of young girls have been arguing with the supervisor recently and she thinks it is time to impose more discipline. She also believes that all this talk about equal rights for women is only an excuse to get out of doing work. As a successful businesswoman herself, no one could accuse her of sexism!

Maeve

Maeve doesn't see why her request should be seen as a 'privilege'. She thinks it ought to be her right. If management refuses she will look for another job.

Glossary of Terms

All-Out Strike

A union representing one group of workers in a workplace may seek the support of other unions in order to make strike action more effective. The union at the centre of the dispute may apply to the ICTU for an 'All-Out Picket'. If the ICTU grants such a picket it gives the union concerned the full backing of the trade union movement for the strike.

Closed Shop

This term is used to describe a situation where union membership is a condition of employment. There are two kinds of closed shop, pre-entry and post-entry. Where 'pre-entry' applies, a person has to be a member of a particular trade union before being employed. A 'post-entry' closed shop means that a person already in employment will be required to join a particular union as a result of an agreement between that union and his/her employer.

Collective Bargaining

This terms applies to negotiations between one or more employer/ employer organisations and one or more trade unions, with a view to reaching agreement.

Conciliation

A procedure by which parties in dispute can meet to sort out their differences with the help of a third party.

Craft Union

A union catering for one or more crafts and which has members in different firms.

Federated Union of Employers

An organisation which represents employers, individually or collectively, in negotiations at both local and national level.

General Union

A union which caters for a variety of different categories of workers and may cater for every worker employed in a particular establishment.

150

Irish Congress of Trade Unions

The national trade union centre in Ireland representing over 80 trade unions, with 660,000 members, in both the Republic of Ireland and Northern Ireland.

Industrial Relations Officer

An official of the Labour Court who is mainly concerned with the provision of a conciliation service in the event of an industrial dispute.

Injunction

This is an order to wrongdoers to do something or, more commonly, to stop doing something. When an employer takes picketers to court, he will usually be looking for an injunction that they will stop picketing. The court has jurisdiction to grant injunctions in all cases in which it appears to be just or convenient to make such an order.

The Labour Court

A body established by the Dail to provide machinery for investigating trade disputes. The court consists of a Chairperson and ordinary members representing trade union and employer organisations.

Official Industrial Action

A withdrawal of labour, undertaken by workers with the approval of their union, to persuade a firm to make concessions in respect of improvements in wages or conditions of employment.

Picket

Workers in dispute with their employer often gather at the approaches to their workplace, usually with placards, to convey information, to other workers or to members of the public, regarding the dispute. This is known as placing a picket on a workplace.

Rights Commissioner

A person appointed by the Minister for Labour to assist in the settlement of disputes which affect only one or a small number of workers.

Shop Steward

A union workplace representative who is elected by workers to represent them in accordance with the rules of a union.

Trade Union

An organisation of workers with the main task of negotiating improvements in the wages and conditions of employment and protecting them from unfair decisions of management.

Unofficial Industrial Action
A withdrawal of labour which does not have the approval of the union which represents the workers involved.

White-collar Union
A union which organises clerical, administrative and technical workers who are traditionally deemed by the nature of their work, to be in white-collar (non-manual) employment.